Being Patrick Swayne

Being Patrick Swayye

Essential Teachings from the Master of the Mullet

Neal E. Fischer

Illustrated by Kyle Hilton

CHRONICLE BOOKS
SAN FRANCISCO

Library of Congress Cataloging-in-Publication Data:

Names: Fischer, Neal E., author.
Title: Being Patrick Swayze : essential teachings from the master of the mullet / Neal E. Fischer.
Description: San Francisco : Chronicle Books, [2021]
Identifiers: LCCN 2021027101 | ISBN 9781797212166 (hardcover)
Subjects: LCSH: Swayze, Patrick. | Swayze, Patrick--Miscellanea.
| Motion picture actors and actresses--United States--
Biography. | Motion pictures--Miscellanea.
Classification: LCC PN2287.S95 F57 2021 | DDC 791.4302/8092--
dc23 LC record available at https://lccn.loc.gov/2021027101

Manufactured in China

10 9 8 7 6 5 4 3 2 1

Chronicle Books LLC
680 Second Street
San Francisco, CA 94107

www.chroniclebooks.com

To Colleen, the Baby to my Johnny, and my biggest fan; to my family and loving group of Outsiders, for your endless support and backing me up in rumbles; and to Swayze, for just being so damn cool.

CONTENTS

ELEMENT 3:

HUNGRY EYES

ELEMENT 4:

PEACEFUL WARRIOR

Introduction

During Miss Daly's fourth grade lessons, I would sneak away to the only working bathroom, sit in the only working stall, and unfold my newest note from Annette, the resident new girl at school and my first love. With her memorable scented ink scribbled on top of lined notebook paper, pre-emoji hearts drawn above the I's, and lengthy sentences about how holding hands at the roller rink is what everyone says "second base" is, Annette would always sign her notes with three simple words that would go on to change the course of my life . . . *To Wong Foo*. Little did I know that those words would kickstart my love affair not with Annette (now happily married with kids to a great guy), but with actor Patrick Swayze, the star of her favorite movie *To Wong Foo, Thanks for Everything! Julie Newmar*.

At that point in my life, I only knew Swayze as Darrel in the film adaptation of *The Outsiders,* the Cool Surfer Guy beating up the Red Hot Chili Peppers guy with Ted Theodore Logan in *Point Break*, and Derek in *Youngblood*, a movie that I wore out on VHS along with *Howard the Duck*. I saw myself in him: a former athlete who had dedicated his life to the arts and wasn't ashamed of it; and a creative soul striving to be the best, do the most, and master any skill. While I knew of my admiration for him, I never fully understood what an icon he was until I saw the reactions on people's faces when merely mentioning his name in conversation or poorly attempting the *Dirty Dancing* lift in public (with a lack of muscle mass, I was always Baby).

I was directing a commercial in Chicago a few years ago and several members of my crew worked on *The Beast*, Swayze's last performance while battling the insurmountable odds of pancreatic cancer. Years later, as we stood around the camera, this crew was still talking about the unforgettable experience of working with Swayze. They said that despite the pain he must have been in, he gave a master class in being a class act on set. He told stories when asked about his famous roles, stood up for the crew, and was the first one on set and last to leave. What sealed the deal for me was when a three-hundred-pound grip with a ZZ Top–inspired beard told me he cried the day Swayze passed away. If that isn't proof of Swayze's staying power, I don't know what is.

I could go on and on about how Swayze has impacted my life or how I reference *Road House* in almost every episode of my podcast, but that's not why you're here. You've picked up this book because you're already a fan. Or a recent convert. Perhaps you don't know anything about Swayze and are interested in learning more about the Master of the Mullet. Whatever the case may be, you have opened yourself up to teachings that will transform your life, fun and games that will make you smile, and overdue admiration for a legend gone too soon. Much like the words of Sam Wheat (*Ghost*), "The love inside, you take it with you," I hope you find something inside this book to take with you. To make those long days a little shorter, cold days a little warmer, and provide you with the necessary mojo to grow the most masterful mullet humanly possible. As I bid you adieu, I have but one final request. Please find the appropriate coffee table, bookshelf, or resting place/pedestal to display this scripture of Swayze as nobody . . . nobody puts this book in the corner.

WHO IS

PATRICK SWAYZE?

HOW
DARE
YOU.

But in all seriousness, if you're unfamiliar with the work of one of the most beloved humans in history then you've come to the right place. For here, Swayze is the universal truth. The gold standard of telling off your lover's father right before you bust a move. And the shining example of a quadruple threat who had no business being such a gentleman in everything he did but decided to be one anyway. Whether the following pages prove to be life changing or not, they've been meticulously designed and curated to elicit a pre-scribed response: joy.

Quick Facts

(For the Uninitiated)

1. Born in Houston, Texas, on August 18th, 1952, to engineering draftsman Jesse Wayne Swayze and choreographer/dance instructor Patsy Karnes

2. Accomplished athlete, gymnast, musician, and classically trained dancer who studied in NYC with the Harkness Ballet Company and Joffrey Ballet before becoming a principal dancer with the Eliot Feld Ballet

3. Married teenage sweetheart Lisa Niemi in 1975, who became not only his wife but his creative partner and frequent collaborator on- and off-screen

4. Starred on Broadway, London's West End, and for his first professional gig, performed as Prince Charming in 1972 for the *Disney on Parade* touring arena stage show

5. Three-time Golden Globe nominee for Best Lead Actor in a Motion Picture (*Dirty Dancing, Ghost,* and *To Wong Foo, Thanks for Everything! Julie Newmar*) and known for memorable performances in such films as *The Outsiders*, *Red Dawn*, *Road House*, *Point Break*, and *Donnie Darko*

6. Starred in films that have collectively grossed over $1 billion at the box office

7. *People* magazine's Sexiest Man Alive in 1991 (and Sexiest Man Alive every year in our hearts)

8. Licensed pilot, conservationist, martial artist, and breeder of Egyptian Arabian horses

9. Singer-songwriter whose most famous creation, "She's Like The Wind" (cowritten with Stacy Widelitz), rose to no. 3 on *Billboard*'s Hot 100 and no. 1 on the Adult Contemporary chart

10. Passed away in 2009 after a courageous battle with pancreatic cancer that he fought while filming his final acting performance on the A&E network television show *The Beast*

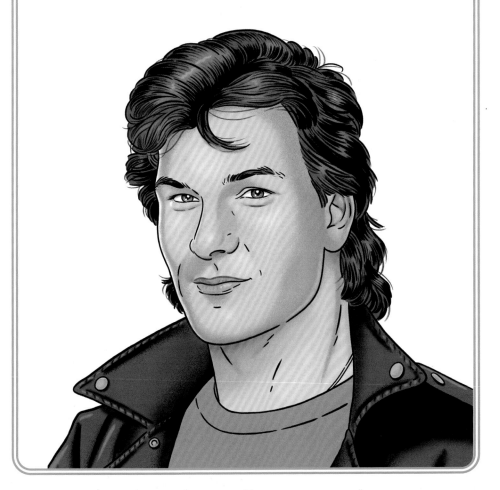

HOW TO USE
This Book

You are about to embark on a treasured collection of essential teachings and principles designed to cultivate your mind, body, and soul. Through the use of movie quotes and cinematic wisdom, physical and mental exercises, games, activities, and quizzes, this journey will unlock your Swayze swagger, leading to a more harmonious life. After you've finished, you'll be impressing friends and strangers alike with your endless knowledge and admiration for one of Hollywood's most likable and underappreciated stars. Not only did he fend off a Russian invasion as a high school student, fight in the Civil War across from his best friend, and help bring his murderer to justice (you get the idea), but for half a century Patrick Swayze has remained in our hearts, on our minds, and is the sole reason that any trip to a vacation resort must first start at the dance hall . . . just in case they employ their own Johnny Castle. Embrace these teachings and achieve newfound clarity in all aspects of your life.

Common Questions About Completing This Course

Q: After I'm done reading, will I dance like Swayze?

A: Don't be silly. People didn't start playing basketball like MJ after watching *The Last Dance*.

Q: Will I become as suave, as handsome, or as charismatic as Swayze?

A: Absolutely not. However, after completion, the blood vessels in your head will magically grow a protein called Swayz-atin and begin force-feeding your roots like Chestnut at Coney Island, resulting in the most glorious of mullets. Don't ask how—it's just science.

Q: Will I have a better understanding of what made Patrick Swayze so special? Or what made him a once-in-a-generation talent that we don't celebrate often enough? Or how to honor him in everyday life?

A: Now that's more like it. The answer is yes to all of those things.

Q: How do you break down the career of Patrick Swayze by separating his essence into bite-size teachable moments that are easy to comprehend?

A: Glad you asked. The best way to study, appreciate, and learn from the Master of the Mullet is by practicing what is known as Feng Swayze.

Q: Is Feng Swayze the same service that costs my Great Aunt Mary Ann fifteen hundred dollars to have a trained consultant rearrange her home?

A: Nope. That's Feng Shui, which for the record is more than just moving furniture around. It's the Chinese art and science that creates harmony and balance in your surrounding environment by cultivating a flow of energy, known as Qi (Chi), to improve your quality of life.

While similar in name, Feng Swayze is the not-so-ancient art of bringing balance to your Patrick Swayze fandom by equally appreciating all the elements that make him the wave-surfing, throat-ripping, dirty-dancing icon that he is. Or, as it's scientifically known, being "crazy for Swayze."

Feng Swayze Elemental Chart

The Feng Swayze Elemental Chart depicts the five elements of Patrick Swayze that you will study throughout this course. Each element represents an avenue of appreciation.

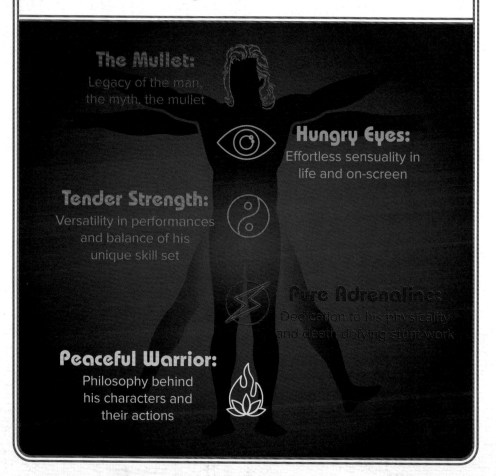

The Mullet:
Legacy of the man, the myth, the mullet

Hungry Eyes:
Effortless sensuality in life and on-screen

Tender Strength:
Versatility in performances and balance of his unique skill set

Pure Adrenaline:
Dedication to his physicality and death-defying stunt work

Peaceful Warrior:
Philosophy behind his characters and their actions

As the most crucial and abundant elements in the universe (sorry, carbon and hydrogen), this quintessential quintet represents the essence and power of Swayze. Sure, purveyors of Feng Shui might argue that their five elements (wood, water, fire, metal, earth) are more important since they are technically the building blocks of life. But what is life without Patrick Swayze?

In the following pages, you will find each element of Swayze broken down alongside lessons and wisdom. When the elements are combined they may not summon The Planeteers, but they'll strike the ultimate balance in paying homage to the humble cowboy himself.

How to Use This Feng Swayze Elemental Chart in Everyday Life

- Tape to your bathroom mirror for daily affirmations
- Place above your computer or near your workspace for inspiration
- Laminate and keep inside your wallet or purse for daily tune-ups
- Hang above your headboard to spice things up in the bedroom
- Tattoo on your solar plexus like Swayze's character Nomad in *Steel Dawn*

Element 1:

TENDER
Strength

LESSON NO. 1:
Find balance in all facets of your life

The first element in appreciating Swayze represents the balance that he carried over from his life into his roles. Not like Johnny Castle balancing on a log, or balancing on a surfboard during the fifty-year storm (RIP Bodhi), but closer to the concept of yin and yang, or contrary forces that are complementary. If you look at the famous roles just mentioned, you can see that they possessed a tender strength. Johnny Castle was street smart and tough but wore his heart on his sleeve. Bodhi had his own Zen surfer philosophy but was a hardened criminal (and yet you wanted to follow him). Swayze himself was equal parts stoic and sensitive, machismo and grace, and possessed just the right amount of swagger and vulnerability not often seen in his cinematic counterparts. Whether he got it from his father, Jesse, whom Swayze referred to as a "gentle cowboy," or he picked it up along the way, achieving balance was no doubt his X factor.

The Swayze Way

Expecting the Unexpected
Since 1979

Swayze's memorable performances are a testament to his unique multifaceted skill set (actor, dancer, athlete, musician) coupled with his commitment to grounding his characters with a level of rawness and emotional resonance that proved to be the secret sauce (nay, Swayze sauce), helping him transcend familiar leading man tropes and elevate projects that now might be considered B-movie material.

Often overlooked or discounted by his eclectic filmography, Swayze fought for many of his most iconic roles. *Ghost* producers didn't want someone with a tough-guy image, so he proved them wrong by giving a nuanced performance as Sam Wheat. *To Wong Foo, Thanks for Everything! Julie Newmar* producers didn't think he could pull off being a drag queen, but as the story goes, with the help of his own makeup team he transformed himself into Vida Boheme during auditions and pulled director Beeban Kidron down a city street, proving he could pass as a woman. Swayze took risks with his projects and forced the audience to "expect the unexpected," just like his *Road House* character Dalton so eloquently taught us. Just take a look at his first four feature films, where he goes from a sexy roller-skating gang leader (*Skatetown, U.S.A.*) to overprotective brother raising a rowdy household (*The Outsiders*), then emotionally scarred soldier (*Uncommon Valor*) to alcoholic demolition derby driver (*Grandview, U.S.A.*). He easily could have taken that first role, rinsed and repeated, and laughed his way to the teen idol bank.

Instead, he kept audiences on their toes by shutting down any perceptions that he was just a heartthrob, just a dancer, or just an action star, which fueled him to constantly flip the script and choose projects that excited him and not the ones expected of him.

That unmatched versatility helped him on many different levels throughout his career, including but not limited to his dance background and inherent athleticism allowing him to easily digest dance and fight choreography, or his stage work preparing him for later in life when he became an effective ensemble member, foregoing the spotlight and just serving the material. These qualities, along with his endless curiosity as an actor, which continued to shine up until his death, helped Swayze build a career of playing good and bad guys, anti-heroes and folk heroes, lovers, fighters, and for once in his career, the inferior dancer to legend Chris Farley on SNL. Were all of his projects box office hits or award-winning films? No. But there's something to be said about ignoring the outside noise, picking projects off gut instinct, and bringing your own brand of charm and, of course, balance, to each role.

And for that, we thank him.

A SWAYZE FOR ALL SEASONS

Did you know that actor Billy Zane almost had the role of Johnny Castle in *Dirty Dancing*? Thankfully, Swayze stepped in and forever warmed our hearts because while Zane may have given a captivating performance, his dance moves would have been (to borrow a word from his character Cal Hockley in *Titanic*) totally blasé. How would you have felt seeing *Ghost* with an on-screen performance between then-married couple Demi Moore and Bruce Willis? Well, before Swayze had us unleashing the water-works in theaters, Willis turned down the role because he didn't like the idea of playing a character that's dead the entire time. Actors nearly missing out on or straight-up turning down parts in films that end up becoming massive successes is as consistent as death and taxes, or Hollywood actors not paying taxes.

Let's take a look at some roles that almost became part of the Swayze saga.

LETHAL WEAPON (1987)

Swayze was just one name on a laundry list of Hollywood stars considered for the role of Martin Riggs, made famous by Mel Gibson. Swayze might not have fought a shirtless Gary Busey in a slippery fire hydrant brawl on Roger Murtaugh's front lawn, but he'd costar with him in *Point Break* a few years later.

TANGO & CASH (1989)

Swayze was slated to star alongside Sylvester Stallone as Gabriel Cash but dropped out to make *Road House* instead. The part ultimately went to Kurt Russell, the only other man who can pull off a proper mullet.

TOTAL RECALL (1990)

If only Rekall was a real company, we could implant memories of the never-made version of this film with Swayze. But instead of a buff construction worker, Swayze's Douglas Quaid would have been more of an accountant-type. His director would not have been Dutch cinematic satirist Paul Verhoeven but rather Australian Bruce Beresford, director of 1989's *Driving Miss Daisy*. The finished version with Arnold Schwarzenegger would ultimately have no Swayze and Sharon Stone fight scene (bummer), or Swayze and Michael Ironside fight scene (double bummer), but would bless us with the haunting image of Arnold suffocating on Martian air with noises that can only be described as the wail of an electrocuted wombat.

PREDATOR 2 (1990)

After suffering some injuries on *Road House*, Swayze traded in a pistol for a pottery wheel in *Ghost*. While it would have been fun to see him join Bill Paxton and Gary Busey again, we got our money's worth by seeing a Predator speak out loud with catchphrases like, "Shit happens!"

ZOMBIELAND (2009)

This film features one of the most memorable cameos in recent history with actor Bill Murray playing a version of himself (in a very Bill Murrian way) uninfected by the virus but pretending to be a zombie. The original draft of the script had Patrick Swayze in this role, but unlike Murray, he would have been an actual zombie. The role was never offered to him, as he had just begun his fight with cancer, but seeing Swayze bite his teeth into this cameo alongside the talented cast would have been a blast.

Movie Meditations

The Swayze Filmography Pairing Guide

Some people chant, others focus on breathing, and a select few choose to listen to thrash metal in a pitch-black room, but when it comes to meditating on the career of Patrick Swayze, there's no better place to start than by watching his filmography from start to finish. From his subdued and tender performances to the explosive action scenes and memorable lines, these transcendental movie meditations will aid you in your quest to create the proper balance of all things Swayze and educate you on why he was so special.

Along with a completed list of Swayze's films (and select TV appearances), you will be provided with some suggested food and/or drink pairings to fully enhance your viewing experience. Now find a comfortable position, clear your mind, take a deep breath, and let the power of Swayze wash over you.

Skatetown, U.S.A.

=== 1979 ===

Swayze, Chachi, Marcia Brady, and sexy roller-skating? Say no more! After a few sips of lukewarm soda handed to you by an apathetic teenager, preheat the oven for a Fresh Herb Pizza. Before sprinkling your preferred "herb" on top like the concession stand in the film, make sure it's legally scrumptious first.

Tidbit: Swayze's first feature film role that utilized his former competitive roller-skating skills.

The Outsiders

=== 1983 ===

To get in the spirit of watching this seminal book come to life, use some hydrogen peroxide to dye your hair blonde, and immediately slick it back as you read a few chapters of *Gone With The Wind*. Chow down on a BBQ chicken sandwich followed by an entire chocolate cake, washed down with a bottle of beer for dessert.

Uncommon Valor

=== 1983 ===

In honor of Swayze's memorable fight scene with costar Randall "Tex" Cobb, find your spiciest and most flavorful Tex-Mex joint and go to town. During that fight scene, take a bite out of a hot pepper each time Swayze lands a punch and make sure to keep a glass of milk nearby. The only thing hotter than your taste buds will be watching a mustached Gene Hackman for two hours.

Tidbit: Gene Hackman didn't just play a Marine—he was one! He left home at sixteen and lied about his age to enlist. Oscar-winner Hackman took Swayze under his wing on set and taught the burgeoning star lessons he would carry with him for his entire career. Class act!

Grandview, U.S.A.

1984

This coming-of-age story from *Grease* director Randal Kleiser is true '80s Americana. What's more American than a slice of apple pie? For the full Cody's Speedrome demolition derby experience, enjoy that delicious dessert with a corn dog!

Tidbit: Speaking of *Grease*, Swayze portrayed Danny Zuko on Broadway for an eight-month stint starting in 1978, only a few months before friend John Travolta's version landed on-screen.

Red Dawn

1984

To prepare for World War III, procure some warm deer blood after a fresh kill, or as it's known in the film, "Spirit of The Deer." If you can't or won't kill a deer, V8 juice or a Bloody Mary is totally fine. Make sure to watch in the morning and eat Beef Stroganoff, so you can be like Swayze and eat Russians for breakfast.

North and South, Book I;
North and South, Book II

1985/1986

Swayze's portrayal of Orry Main, Confederate Army soldier and southern gentleman, sent his career soaring. This epic miniseries gives you twelve hours to soak up Swayze. In return for this gift, you must also wear a heavy woolen uniform in the sun to soak up your sweat. For your troubles, enjoy a nice glass of Southern Comfort with a side of South Carolina boiled peanuts.

Youngblood

1986

Since the film takes place in Toronto, you'll want to eat a signature Torontonian dish: a peameal bacon sandwich with mustard. Wash it down with a cold Canadian beer or hot tea. As Swayze's character Derek says, "The only thing better than a glass of beer is tea with Miss McGill!"

Dirty Dancing

1987

Friends don't let friends be the type of person who HASN'T seen *Dirty Dancing*. Get a group together and munch on "Penny's Mambo Cuban Sandwich," which is just a normal Cuban sandwich but holds the pickles and leaves the hard stuff to Johnny. To quench your thirst after staring at the ultimate thirst trap for two hours, a Watermelon Margarita is your best friend.

Steel Dawn

1987

Ever dreamed of seeing Swayze take an outdoor bath while doing a scene at the same time? You're in luck. To truly pay homage to this film, travel to the Namib Desert, and, in between sword fights, create a special water filtration system with your new love.

Tidbit: This marks the first time Swayze acted in a movie with his wife, Lisa Niemi. She portrays Kasha, a widowed mother living in the desert who falls in love with a traveling warrior, Nomad (Swayze).

Tiger Warsaw

1988

This dark, dramatic turn for Swayze was filmed in and around the blue-collar steel mill town of Sharon, Pennsylvania. Local favorites like Quaker Steak & Lube or Primanti Brothers have been fueling hardworking locals for decades on a hearty diet of meat, cheese, and potatoes. Pair the heavy subject matter with a heavy meal of your own. For dessert? A cozy nap.

Road House

1989

Like a fasting monk, Dalton doesn't eat during the movie and you won't either. However, he does drink coffee. Take yours the same way he takes his: black and leaded (caffeinated).

Next of Kin

1989

To celebrate the on-screen display of Old Testament revenge, take revenge on your liver by having a shot of Chicago's legendary Malort in the pouring rain. What is Malort? If you've had it, you'll never forget it. If you haven't, anyone who has will force you to try it. One thing's for sure, you might forget the night before, but the taste, like a measles vaccine, will last a lifetime.

Ghost

1990

Before JT permanently brought sexy back in 2006, the iconic pottery scene to the tune of *Unchained Melody* did it better. Embrace the Hollywood cliché by eating Chinese food out of the carton while sitting on the floor of your new place. Inviting your future mortal enemy is optional but not recommended (unless it's the actual Tony Goldwyn, who is delightful).

Tidbit: The Righteous Brothers's massive hit used during the pottery scene wasn't the first time Swayze moved appendages to their music. You might remember a little song from *Dirty Dancing* called, "(I've Had) The Time of My Life," which was performed by Righteous Brothers member Bill Medley and vocalist Jennifer Warner. Now you have two classics stuck in your head!

Point Break

1991

To eat: Surf 'n' Turf. Natch. To drink: a "Vaya Con Dos Equis" or double-fisting bottles of Dos Equis. Or, if you don't partake in alcohol, substitute it with a "Vaya Con Café Con Leche" instead. If a guest goes full Gary Busey by the end of the night, document it first, then grab them an Uber or a Lyft.

Tidbit: The film was directed by cinematic badass Kathryn Bigelow, the first woman to win the Academy Award for Best Director for her work on the 2009 film *The Hurt Locker.*

The Player

1992

Swayze's cameo was unfortunately cut from the finished film. Follow these directions:

- Buy the Criterion Collection Blu-ray.
- In the Menu, go to Supplementals.

Voila! You can now see the deleted scene where Swayze wears medical scrubs and debates the merits of Eastern vs. Western martial arts with actor Fred Ward.

Like a Hollywood working lunch on the company card, it's completely within reason that you'll plan to eat something but don't touch your food.

City of Joy

1992

From the director of *The Killing Fields,* this film follows a distraught surgeon traveling to India in search of spiritual enlightenment. It might deal with heavy subject matter, but you should focus on a light and tasty meal like the celebrated street food of Kolkata: phuchka, beguni, or kati rolls.

Father Hood

1993

Curate a mixture of the best unhealthy snacks and drinks that roadside convenience stores can offer and drive on the highway while your kids (or those happily provided by close friends or family) scream at you for the duration of the film. For even more texture, invite an octogenarian Vegas gambler to sit shotgun and smoke while making prop bets on road-kill sightings.

Tall Tale

1995

For period-appropriate Wild West smells, refrain from showering for at least five to seven days before watching this film. A proper musk is needed to truly enjoy the tallness of this tale. The perfect meal consists of warm whiskey and chewing on blue Beef Jerky.

To Wong Foo, Thanks For Everything! Julie Newmar

1995

Any viewing of this classic must begin by having "a day with the girls," where you and your friends glam up from head to toe in preparation for your own Strawberry Social! As Noxeema says, "Red and wild. That's your theme!" Rouge up your surroundings, put on your dancing shoes, and bake a fresh strawberry pie to eat in between sips of Strawberry Daiquiris!

Tidbit: A well-documented story from the set saw stars Patrick Swayze and John Leguizamo almost come to blows over a disagreement about sticking to the script.

Three Wishes

1995

Put up the projection screen, raise the tent, and bust out the bug spray because this movie is best viewed outside while camping and eating the "On McCloud Nine" smores named after Swayze's character, Jack McCloud. The supersized smores consist of three graham crackers, three pieces of chocolate, and three marshmallows.

Black Dog

1998

This action-packed Swayze film sees him driving heavy machinery with his own heavy machinery (his muscular arms). After chugging an energy drink for the long haul, chew on some homemade meatloaf while watching actor/musician Meat Loaf chew all the scenery around him.

Letters from a Killer

Swayze's character interacts with pen pals from prison through a series of tape-recorded love letters. Forego any specific food or drink pairing by recording your own tape-recorded love letters—two to be sent to your favorite restaurants (the more flowery the prose the better) and one to someone you love.

Tidbit: In a very scary moment on set during a stunt, Swayze was thrown off his horse into a tree at high speed. He broke both legs and detached four tendons in his shoulder.

Forever Lulu

Head on over to your local frozen yogurt shop and push past the teens to grab any one of their delicious treats representing the Sugary Sweetness of Melanie Griffith, the Spiciness of Patrick Swayze, or the Everything Nice of Penelope Ann Miller and Joseph Gordon-Levitt.

Green Dragon

A feel-good movie needs some feel-good foods. Whip up some Green Goddess dressing to dip in as many green vegetables as possible while wearing the color green. For you more adventurous viewers, a Green Dragon is an alcoholic drink containing a cannabis concentrate that might very well have you seeing an actual green dragon. Watch responsibly.

Donnie Darko

Muster all your gusto and get your attitudinal beliefs in order by setting aside time on October 2nd to sit back, relax, and enjoy a large plate of Hasenpfeffer. For our friends who have rabbits for pets, substitute pizza for the stew and enjoy a polite discourse about parenting, taxes, and onetime presidential hopeful Michael Dukakis with your family.

Tidbit: The infomercial for Swayze's character, Jim Cunningham, was filmed on the ranch that he shared with wife Lisa Niemi. Swayze gave them the use of his actual clothes from the '80s to fully realize the character.

Waking Up in Reno

Feeling adventurous? Attempt to go bite for bite with Billy Bob Thornton's character, Lonnie Earl, by eating a seventy-two-ounce steak and all the trimmings in under an hour. Or as Swayze's character, Roy, calls it, "The Ass End of a Rhino." It probably wouldn't hurt to have an ambulance nearby.

One Last Dance

Feast on a dancer's meal of baked salmon, greens, butternut squash, and for dessert, dark chocolate that is at least 90% cocoa. If you really want to be one with the dancers, after each on-screen dance performance, alternate ice packs over your aching muscles to fully appreciate the painstakingly difficult performance they went through for your enjoyment.

Tidbit: Lisa Niemi wrote and directed the film, which is based on the play *Without a Word* cowritten and performed in 1984 by Niemi, Swayze, and Nicholas Gunn.

11:14

2003

This twist-heavy indie black comedy has multiple storylines featuring a talented cast of stars and future household names. For optimum results, press play at 11:14 PM on November 14th, and then proceed to eat eleven almonds (for health reasons) and fourteen chocolate chips (for fun reasons).

Dirty Dancing: Havana Nights

2004

He might not be playing Johnny Castle, but you still get a cameo from vintage Swayze playing a dance teacher in this film set during the Cuban revolution. To offset the palpable heat that oozes off the screen, dance your way toward the oldest cocktail in Cuba, the Canchanchara.

King Solomon's Mines

2004

As you watch adventurer Allan Quartermain search unexplored regions, adventure to the depths of your refrigerator to find usable and unexpired ingredients so you can whip together a comfort dish from your imagination.

George and the Dragon

2004

Find a medieval-era longsword (or garden-variety kitchen knife), chop up half a dozen spicy dragon wings (or buffalo wings), add them to your giant dragon egg omelet (or two to three regular eggs), and garnish it with a sprinkle of coagulated dragon's milk (cheese), and you've got a meal fit for a knight of the kitchen table.

Keeping Mum

2005

To truly appreciate Maggie Smith as a problem-solving house-keeper with a flair for murder, it makes the most sense to have a civilized portion of biscuits (preferably Cornish Fairings), along with a cup of hot tea (preferably Earl Grey with a bit of milk), as you'll be getting a healthy portion of Swayze's biscuits during his hilarious thong scene. Yes, thong.

The Fox and the Hound 2

2006

What better dish to snack on during an animated film about dogs than perennial favorite Puppy Chow Mix. This snackable finger food is always a hit at parties and seems to remain in snack rotation for at least a week. For extra fun, challenge guests to do their best Reba McEntire impression (Swayze's costar) with a mouth full of the mix and let the hilarity ensue.

Christmas in Wonderland

2007

With the majority of this film taking place in a mall, you'll get the most bang for the buck by picking up a variety pack of food court delicacies. For dessert, your best bet is homemade cookies with frosting portraits of costars Tim Curry, Chris Kattan, and Carmen Electra.

Jump!

2008

Not a filmed adaptation of the Van Halen classic, but a period courtroom drama based on a true story! Stop over at your local thrift store and pick up the best suit and fedora you can find to join in on Swayze's suaveness. The trial takes place in Innsbruck, Austria, where you'd be hard-pressed to find a cuter patio to visit than at Fischerhausl (for obvious reasons). Watching at home? Indulge in some decadent palatschinken or Austrian crêpes with a cup of coffee.

Powder Blue

2009

Conventional wisdom might tell you that Christmas Eve is a time to spend with family, but Swayze supersedes conventional wisdom. *Powder Blue* takes place on Christmas Eve, which means you must watch it on Christmas Eve. Eat a dozen powdered donuts (blue if you can find them), followed by an hour of intense calisthenics and an aerobic pole dancing class to gain an appreciation for the skill and strength that Jessica Biel displayed along with a newfound respect for all the professional exotic dancers who do this for a living.

The Beast

This is Swayze's final performance, playing the unorthodox FBI agent Charles Barker, who toes the line between right and wrong, and it is the simplest pairing of all. Take a glass of any beverage and raise it high to salute Patrick Swayze for working his ass off while fighting one hell of a disease and still, above all, delivering a powerful performance. Cheers to you, Sir.

Choose Your Own Swayze Blockbuster

Ever thought of writing your own Swayze movie? Tried screen-writing but gave up due to the eventual sea of rejection? Well, you're in luck. Taking inspiration from Swayze's particular set of skills (sorry, Liam Neeson) and combining that with the explosive-ness of a classic summer blockbuster, this game featuring unique prompts lets you create an original synopsis for the most epic never-made Swayze flick!

Patrick Swayze stars as Jack " _____ " Wilson, a
　　　　　　　　　　　　　　　　　　　 NOUN

retired _____ and special forces soldier living the
　　　　 OCCUPATION

quiet life in _____ by selling handmade
　　　　　　　 VACATION SPOT

_____ during the day, and restoring his vintage
PLURAL NOUN

_____ in the evening. During his daily
MODE OF TRANSPORTATION

regimen of shirtless _____, and casual read-
　　　　　　　　　　 TYPE OF EXERCISE

ing of PhD-level _____, he is interrupted by his
　　　　　　　　 TYPE OF STUDY

former commanding officer, Rufus _____
TYPE OF BIRD (MOVIE
_____. After partaking in a little _____,
STAR)   ACTIVITY FOR TWO PEOPLE
followed by Jack whipping up his famous _____,
FOOD
Rufus informs Jack that his niece, _____, un-
FEMALE NAME
knowingly ignited a turf war by accidentally grabbing

the wrong suitcase at the airport, which belonged to

the _____ crime family, led by Jack's former lover
LAST NAME
_____ and discovered that it contained the
FLOWER (ACTRESS)
dead _____ of the infamous "_____" Boys
ANIMAL   ALCOHOL BRAND
Gang and the head of a crime syndicate boss.

With Jack's niece held hostage in between warring

factions, Rufus convinces him to strap on his lucky

_____ for one last job. Jack assembles his former
USEFUL ITEM
team, known in black ops as _____. They are
BAND NAME
comprised of _____, a _____ expert, their
NATURAL DISASTER   WEAPON
fraternal twin _____, the enforcer of the
CITY + TOOL
group played by _____ in their first film role, and
MUSICIAN
actor Sam Elliott, playing a version of himself with the

power to magically _____ while reading minds.
CHORE/TASK

In order to prevent World War _____, Jack wages a
NUMBER

personal vendetta against his enemies by risking

everything to infiltrate the secret headquarters of

_____in _____ by breaking through
CHAIN RESTAURANT   FOREIGN CITY

the most highly sophisticated security system designed

by _____. The final test sees Jack attempt to seduce
A GENIUS

his former lover by performing the perfect _____
TYPE OF

_____ in front of a crowd of _____, all while timed
DANCE   PLURAL NOUN

explosives are strapped to his _____.
BODY PART

With a series of twists and turns, this blockbuster

extravaganza that _____ calls "unforgettable" has
CELEBRITY

Patrick Swayze achieving his most _____ stunts
ADJECTIVE

ever as he _____ over the _____
EXTREME SPORT   MONUMENT

blindfolded, engages in a horseback chase around

_____, performs a passionate love scene
TOURIST ATTRACTION

inside a _____, and has a DeNiro/Pacino–like acting
PLACE

face-off with _____ as they play a tense and compet-
ACTOR
itive round of _____ while reading _____ at the
BOARD GAME   BOOK
same time.

Featuring an original song by Patrick Swayze titled

"_____," don't miss _____'s film,
LAST TEXT YOU SENT   FILM DIRECTOR
"Project _____: The Battle for _____"!
MYTHOLOGICAL NAME   NOUN

In theaters this _____!
SEASON

**Once complete use your best movie
trailer voice to perform your finished Swayze
Blockbuster for friends and family.**

Element 2:

PURE
Adrenaline

LESSON NO. 2:
Embrace fear and overcome it

Under a magical desert sunrise with his sun-soaked locks bouncing in the wind, *Point Break*'s Bodhi gives a parachute to Johnny Utah and says, "Pure adrenaline, right? The ultimate rush. Other guys snort for it, jab a vein for it, all you gotta do is jump." That memorable line was about jumping out of an airplane (also applicable for nieces and nephews who won't go in the pool), but Bodhi's fearlessness and search for the ultimate ride was a trait that Swayze shared with his Zen-tagonist creation. He had a personal quest for perfection throughout his life, like achieving peak human condition with his physicality or his commitment to stunt work (with many broken bones to prove it). He's the shining example of carpe diem and the reason it should be renamed Swayze Diem to "Swayze the Day" or live life to the fullest. Our lives could use a little more Pure Adrenaline, which is why it's the second element in admiring Swayze.

The Swayze Method

Blood, Sweat, Tears, and Stunts

From a young age, Swayze possessed a daredevil-may-care attitude that saw him gleefully jumping off roofs into perfect landings or running around Texas playing Tarzan with his brother, actor Don Swayze. Speaking of our favorite legendary loincloth, let's take a moment to appreciate how perfect a Swayze-led Tarzan film would have been with all the smoldering, acrobatics, and long hair blowing from vine-to-vine as he held Jane for safety! The hero that Swayze idolized the most, however, was pulp heroic adventurer Doc Savage (widely considered a source of inspiration to both Batman and Superman), who was an ordinary man with an extraordinary skill set (martial artist, scientist, explorer, etc.), physically gifted like Tarzan, and mentally skilled like Sherlock Holmes. With Swayze's never-wavering focus and perfectionism in everything he did, it's no surprise why he loved Savage. He shared a fearlessness with that hero that would lead to a love of doing stunts well before his costar in *The Outsiders*, Tom Cruise, became famous for a similar thrill-seeking acting approach, albeit with much more running.

Take a deep dive into some of his most popular films and you'll be astonished to learn that Swayze was often injured despite his pitch-perfect performances. He insisted on doing the majority of surfing (with a few broken ribs to show for it) and skydiving in *Point Break*, the latter of which was stopped by producers over risk concerns. *Dirty Dancing* had Swayze needing his knee drained (which happened multiple times over his career, with his leg almost amputated early on), but on film you would never know. Performing less than 100% and turning in an epic performance is often called a "Jordan flu game," and a "Swayze injury" is a career-ending injury for most mortals, but Swayze treated it like a bump in the road, somehow coming back bigger, faster, and stronger.

In 1989's *Road House,* Swayze's character, Dalton, is read a list of injuries sustained over his life, "You may add nine staples to your dossier of thirty-one broken bones, two bullet wounds, nine puncture wounds, and four stainless steel screws." To be clear, Swayze wasn't a bionic man, but that extravagant estimate isn't far off from the truth. With injuries haunting him over his career, his fearlessness never wavered as he kept fighting back to be the best version of himself off-screen to give us the best version of himself on-screen. That ability to transform fear into an advantage was a skill no doubt learned when facing adversity in junior high as a young male dancer and musician in Texas. One particular beating at the hands of five boys proved to be a turning point for Swayze as it led him to martial arts, as well as being trained by his father, Jesse, a former boxer, on how to defend himself. This all culminated when Jesse and the school's football coach organized a fair fight in the weight room (it was a different time) and Swayze came face-to-face with the same five boys who terrorized him months earlier—but this time, he could face them one-on-one, ultimately finishing the fight by dispatching them all.

If something could be learned, Swayze learned it. If something could be conquered, Swayze conquered it. Whether it was jumping out of a plane or flying a plane, learning to fight or fighting the waves, no challenge was too big for him. That endless ambition, focus, and passion for perfection, or pure adrenaline, gave us a star that we not only looked up at on the big screen but someone we always looked up to in the way he carried himself.

Sweatin' Like Swayze

The Workout

Remember late-night infomercial fitness fads? If we're all being honest, our basements are likely chock full of contraptions and cassettes that are collecting enough dust to make a coin collector blush. Three easy payments of $19.99 (plus shipping and handling, of course) and we had buns of steel, Jazzercised our way to Tae Bo, and mastered our thighs with the mom from *Step by Step*. Swayze, on the other hand, didn't need poorly constructed machines to look like he was sculpted from clay. Frequent costar Rob Lowe (a member of the unofficial never-age club with Paul Rudd, J. Lo, and Halle Berry) calls him an Adonis. So what's stopping the rest of us mere mortals? Sure, he had countless years of dance and gymnastics training and genetics seemingly whipped up by a Michelin star chef, but Swayze's fitness success was due to his unmatched work ethic in the gym and staying in tune with his body.

That's why you're going to add these unproven but passionately compiled Swayze-inspired exercises to your regular exercise routine for the most complete workout that is 100% guaranteed to have your heart beating, your blood pumping, and your mouth breathing.

CHEST/SHOULDERS

Shrug off mullet haters with shoulder shrugs

3 sets of 10 with 5-lb kettle bells wearing a wig (unless you're already sporting a mullet, in which case, carry on)

To confirm, you are shrugging off haters and the kettle bells are wearing mullets. Why? If you need to ask, you've already failed.

Golden Globe push-ups

3 sets of 20 while balancing on 24-karat gold-plated bronze globes

To atone for the Hollywood Foreign Press's grave mistake ('88, '91, '96) add twenty-four pounds on your back representing the weight of the three Golden Globe Awards Swayze deserved.

Dirty Dancing lifts

3 sets of 12 reps on land, in water, or near disapproving fathers

Substitute Baby for an actual baby. Bibs are encouraged.

Side splits on two galloping steeds

Maintain splits on one mile of smooth terrain

No horses? Do a plank on your dining room table while wearing a cowboy hat and listening to the soundtrack of *Tall Tale*. Isolate your core.

Extreme skydiving gymnastics

Flip repeatedly in a pike position for abdominal development

If funds are tight, hang upside down on monkey bars as a landscaper hits you with a leaf blower.

Chippendales-inspired full-body pelvic thrusting

20 minutes at any standard garden party

Add extra resistance by wearing a belt adorned with six suburban dad cell phone holsters.

LEGS/CARDIO

Disco roller skate lunges

5 laps with quad skates. Shirt optional, leather vest mandatory

Get extra back mobility by unbuckling your belt and stretching while mimicking a sexy lion tamer.

FBI foot chase through Los Angeles

60 minutes on the treadmill (7% incline; 100% inclination)

Wear a Halloween mask and pretend to run from a dreamy Keanu Reeves.

Jump! Jumping jacks

3 sets of 100 jacks in a three-piece suit

If you're a Missourian (jumping jacks are the official state exercise), take a breather and ring out the sweat from your suit. You've earned it.

Steamy consensual love to Motown hits

Passionate cardio from treadmill to mattress

Going solo? Jump on a rowing machine for thirty minutes. Follow with a steam room where nude old-timers tell you about "real music."

Sweatpants Tai Chi

60 minutes shirtless and sweaty while enemies stare in resentful longing

To freshen up your routine, do the choreography to Psy's "Gangnam Style" in super slow motion.

Perform a pas de deux to perfection

4 movements from Tchaikovsky's "The Nutcracker"

Not into ballet? Dance with a life-size Nutcracker to the entirety of The Verve's "Bitter Sweet Symphony."

ARMS

A Civil War saber fencing assault (duel)

Period-inappropriate hairstyle a must

Since you were going to ask anyway, yes, a lightsaber works too.

Tall Tale your triceps

30 minutes of rip-snorting lasso work on each arm

Want to speak a love language to your mate? Lasso dirty laundry while riding a Dyson Cyclone vacuum cleaner around the house.

Self-defense throat rips

3 sets of 5 at dusk near bodies of water

Duct tape raw chicken cutlets to a mannequin. Isolate biceps. Rip. Sanitize. Tape. Repeat.

THE
OFFICIAL
Road House
DRINKING
GAME

Get ready for mullets, explosions, and heel kicks to the face unlike any drinking game in the known universe. Prepare your body for an immersive experience based on Patrick Swayze's most epic and rewatchable creation, director Rowdy Herrington's 1989 classic, *Road House*.

This is a film that after three decades of being released sits atop *Variety's* 2020 list of "100 Movies That Saved Cable" due to how much it's replayed on television. Turn on your TV right now and it's probably on. If you're reading this and haven't seen *Road House* you should be ashamed that you haven't exposed your eyeballs to a modern western in the spirit of classics like *Shane* cloaked in the neon glow of a dying era. Embarrassed that you've overlooked a movie featuring a part-time pacifist and bouncer with a degree in philosophy (oh yes, you read that right) that stops at nothing to defend the little guy being taken advantage of in a corrupt Missouri town? Gather your friends, oil up those muscles, and throw your car keys in the bowl because it's time to play The Official *Road House* Drinking Game!

Disclaimer: This game is designed to be a complementary and optional experience to enjoy the film with friends. Please drink/play responsibly, or like unruly customers of Dalton's, you'll be taken out with the trash.

THE OFFCIAL

Road House

DRINK MENU

Jasper's Finest

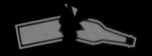

Any bottle of ice-cold beer

So many bottles are broken over tables and heads at The Double Deuce that drinking a cold one will have you fitting right in. Don't fret over brands or styles of beer; by the end of this game your stomach and toilet bowl won't know the difference between an IPA or a Pilsner.

The Throat Ripper Shot

1/3 oz. tequila
1/3 oz. whiskey
1/3 oz. Goldschlager cinnamon schnapps
1 drop of Tabasco sauce
(2 if adventurous, 3 if you're a glutton for punishment)

The signature shot of the night is based on the throat rip heard 'round the world and should be consumed at that very moment. To appreciate the sight of one man ripping out another man's throat in self-defense, you must subject your own throat to an unbearable burning sensation. Razor for spontaneous hair growth is not included.

The Mijo Mojito

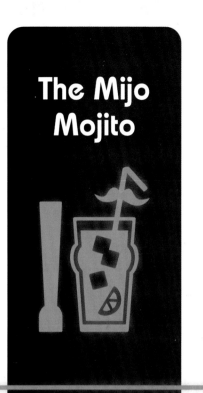

Fresh mint leaves
1 lime, cut into wedges
1 tbsp. agave syrup
2 oz. white rum
Soda water
Ice
Mustache straw
Sam Elliott accent (optional)

Inspired by Wade's term of endearment for Dalton, this Mojito recipe is an old-school classic just like the man who taught Dalton everything he knows. Place three lime wedges in a highball glass along with some mint leaves and your agave. Using your biceps, and displaying them for all to see, muddle the mixture until the oils are released along with whistles of excitement from fellow partygoers. Add ice, then the rum, soda water to the top, and your last lime for garnish. Place in your mustache straw and stir to enjoy.

The Leaded Libation

Cold brew coffee (aka Cooler Brew)
2 oz. whiskey
1 oz. simple syrup
Ice
Splash of cream (optional)

When Dalton works long hours at The Double Deuce you're likely to find him standing by the bar with a cup of leaded (caffeinated) coffee in his hand and a focus on the action. His mind, like his reflexes, must stay sharp. This recipe is no-frills just like the man who inspired it. Pick any type of glass, mug, or even mason jar and fill it with ice. Drop in your whiskey, your simple syrup, and pour that deliciously buzz-worthy cold brew to the top. Add a splash of cream if you'd like some extra sweetness, stir, and enjoy!

Take a Sip When...

If you're not a drinker, do your tolerance a favor
and ignore any bolded moments.

You hear the name Dalton

Tilghman creepy smiles (you'll know it when you see it)

Someone comments on Dalton's size or says they thought he'd be bigger

Tilghman brings some class back to his establishment by cleverly turning a "Fuck" into a "Buick" with his handy marker

There is gratuitous nudity

A knife is pulled on Dalton; two sips for when he's cut

A beer bottle breaks during a fight (be careful with this one)

Dalton fires someone

Someone messes with Dalton's work vehicle

Someone says "Double Deuce"; two sips for "Double Douche"

Dalton lights a cigarette

The tablecloth dress makes an appearance

Dalton shuts down a tense moment with a quip or one-liner

When you hear the line, "Calling me sir is like putting an elevator in an outhouse. It don't belong."

Wesley is in a new form of transportation

The band leader Cody (Jeff Healey) counts "1, 2, 3, 4"

Dalton lists an important rule during new staff orientation

Wade calls Dalton "Mijo"

When you hear the line "Pain Don't Hurt"

Dalton is shirtless; two sips for his naked behind

Someone stares at Dalton in an overly suggestive manner

Doc hits the rock in the throes of passion

When you hear the line, "I used to fuck guys like you in prison"

Wesley stares across the water at Dalton or his "activities"

A house, business, or vehicle explodes, making claims adjusters sweat.

Popcorn Trivia for Bathroom Breaks

1. In numerous interviews, *The Late Show* host Stephen Colbert admits that he auditioned for the film. No word yet on what character he read for, but just imagining the possibilities is an exciting thought experiment.

2. The character of Red is portrayed by actor/stuntman/musician Red West, who was also well known for his relationship with Elvis Presley. He was a boyhood friend of the singer and member of his "Memphis Mafia," where he held such positions as a personal driver, bodyguard (Red was a Golden Gloves boxer and karate instructor), and even co-songwriter on some of Presley's hits.

3. Sam Elliott revealed in an interview that the original cut of the film was over three hours long, featuring extended scenes. If you seek out the original theatrical trailer online you'll see some of the cut scenes, including Wade raising a beer to Dalton and saying, "So says the fighting philosopher!"

4. During the climactic clash of the titans fight between Dalton and Jimmy you'll notice a moment when Jimmy grabs a stray log and swings it across Swayze's side. While filming, actor Marshall Teague (Jimmy) thought he was grabbing a prop log (otherwise, fake) and swung it as hard as he could, realizing (too late) that the log was very much real. It broke in two and in turn broke some of Swayze's ribs!

5. Perhaps the most famous and entertaining trivia tidbit belongs to Kelly Lynch. Every time her love scene with Swayze is on TV, Bill Murray and his brothers prank call her husband Mitch Glazer (cowriter of *Scrooged*) and tell him, "Kelly is having sex with Patrick Swayze right now!" The multi-decade tradition even spans time zones as Murray once called the couple from Russia. Many viewers are also concerned for her back during this scene as it's being pushed against that rock wall. Don't worry—she was wearing padding, although that didn't protect her from Swayze's rock hard abs.

Connect the Swayze Artwork

Take a deep breath, close your eyes, and clear your mind.

What did you see? If you answered "a hand-drawn shirtless Swayze," then you'd be absolutely right and alarmingly clairvoyant. It's time for your best Enrique Senis-Oliver impression. He was an artist commissioned in 1973 by oil heiress Rebekah Harkness to paint a mural inside her then—brand new Harkness Theatre. Featuring beautifully rendered naked dancers paying homage to Terpsichore, the goddess of dance, most of the poses were done by, you guessed it, Patrick Swayze.

So sharpen those pencils and grab your color palette because you're connecting the dots on a still frame of Swayze's triceps and biceps and traps (Oh my!) for your very own tasteful portrait of the male torso. Eat your heart out, Ingres!

Element 3:

HUNGRY

Eyes

LESSON NO. 3:
Love like there is no tomorrow

Featured in *Dirty Dancing* and named after Eric Carmen's 1987 hit song, Hungry Eyes is the third element in honoring all that is Swayze. Look in any knick-knack shop or midwestern bathroom and next to the scented soap and potpourri you're likely to see a cross-stitch pattern or chiseled rock that says, "The eyes are the window to the soul." Whether it was fading dreams in the eyes of an injured Derek Sutton in *Youngblood*, empathy for his patients as Max Lowe in *City of Joy*, or the romanticism of a southern gentleman in *North and South*, Swayze's eyes weren't just a window to the soul but rather a skylight of sensuality and passion that informed and complemented each of his performances. By displaying a vulnerability that can't be taught, he made those fairy-tale peepers his secret weapon.

The Swayze Gaze

Melting Hearts and Minds

If you're a member of the current generation, you might not understand the cultural impact of Patrick Swayze's broad-reaching sex appeal. Swayze oozed effortless sensuality from every sweating pore on-screen, and despite the media often calling him just a sex symbol (a label he disliked because he thought it took away from his serious acting), he was so much more than that. When he was on-screen the camera finally departed from the typical Hollywood male gaze (coined by filmmaker/scholar Laura Mulvey) and instead represented all gazes, because what set Swayze apart from his peers was the way he seemed to transcend gender norms. Women wanted him and men wanted to be him just as much as men wanted him and women wanted to be him. He had that magical and befuddling quality that every person's crush has had for ages . . . he didn't try too hard. And it was that reluctance and rejection of the sex symbol persona that would ultimately solidify him as . . . well, a sex symbol.

When Frances "Baby" Houseman jogs up a gravel walkway to start that memorable dance montage in *Dirty Dancing*, she is quickly told by Swayze's Johnny to lock her frame, and as their bodies come together, audiences around the globe collectively locked eyes on a magical display of romantic chemistry initiated by Swayze. From the growing attraction between their on-screen characters to real-life giggles of actress Jennifer Grey and the real-life frustration of Swayze when he strokes her arm (true story), we can clearly see how Swayze captivates us with ease and forces us to never look away. In that same montage, he literally gestures with his fingers for Baby to look him in his eyes and, in turn, grabs our unwavering attention too.

Perhaps the best example of Swayze's power is arguably the most famous (or at least most recognizable) love scene in history from *Ghost*. In the clay-drenched hands of anyone else, this scene would have ended up on the cutting-room floor. You'd never know it, but while filming, Swayze's insecurities about living up to his media-adopted persona and his lack of confidence during love scenes weighed on him heavily. But as always, he was true to his performance (with a little help from The Righteous Brothers), and in the end it didn't matter if the film was about sexual awakening in the sixties or a story of love beyond this mortal coil—Swayze played his characters with an unrivaled honesty that he was never commended enough for during his lifetime. Through every performance or public appearance, it was clear; when you looked in those Hungry Eyes, no matter the character, story, or film, staring right back at you was pure love—love for his wife, love for his art, a love for life, and, most importantly, love for his audience.

Fashionably
SWAYZE

Now that you're well on your way to transforming your body, it's time to outfit your new curves with a timeless collection of essential Swayze film ensembles featuring your very own Swayze couture starter kit. Swayze might not have been considered a fashion icon, but his on-screen wardrobe always managed to possess rugged functionality and relatability (true to his Texas roots) that meshed with his own personal style. His straightforward and effortless approach was always camera-ready, from the ranch to the red carpet. With trends constantly changing, and former fads suddenly resurfacing (looking at you, fanny packs), this breakdown of outfit homages will have you dressing to impress and turning heads in no time.

From Roofing to Rumbling

The Outsiders

Functional yet comfortable for a long day of work and a long night of brawling.

1. **Pressed work shirt***: Durable for manual labor. Flexible to show off the guns.

2. **Undershirt**: Minimize workday sweat while maximizing blue-collar sex appeal.

3. **Steel-toed boots**: Protect your toes from heavy objects and the skulls of Socs.

4. **Tight denim jeans**: All-American denim that fits snugly around your all-American ass.

*Swap the work shirt for flannel and add leather fingerless gloves and you're ready to rev up an eighteen-wheeler (*Black Dog)* or open an extremely tight jar lid for a loved one.

From Mountain Blood Feud to Big City Vengeance

Next of Kin

Fighting crime never looked so good or oddly representative of two vastly different cultures.

1. **Wide-brimmed fedora:** So city slickers won't forget your Appalachian roots.

2. **Striped dress shirt + tie**: To balance that delicate line of country vs. Gordon Gecko.

3. **Clip-on suspenders**: Maintain perfect posture while engaging in macho posturing.

4. **Unnecessary ponytail:** Tie it up for business time. Take it down for business time.

From Dance Instruction to Dance Finale

Dirty Dancing

Have the time of your life on hot summer nights with street-tough attire that's dance-floor chic.

1. **Black leather jacket**: Edgy. Sexy. Protective. Just like Johnny Castle himself.

2. **Tight black dress shirt**: Unbuttoned with a sweaty chest > buttoned up and boring.

3. **Tight black dress pants:** Just enough room for any well-timed hip thrusts.

4. **Black dance shoes:** For mashing all the potatoes and doing all the twists.

From the Big Apple to the Strawberry Social

To Wong Foo, Thanks for Everything! Julie Newmar

Approval neither desired nor required, but looking utterly fabulous should never be in question.

1. **Say something hat**: Because every day should be a say something hat day.

2. **Black Chanel skirt suit**: "Simplicity is the keynote of all true elegance." —Coco Chanel

3. **Pearls**: Like internal combustion, it's the ultimate accessory.

4. **French tip manicure**: Vibrant, polished, and sturdy for punching abusive husbands.

From Stage Door to Bank Vault Door

Point Break

Formal wear for every foot chase with your bromantic partner. Set hearts and cars aflame!

1. **Tuxedo:** Acceptable at galas, the theater, or robbing the occasional bank.

2. **White formal gloves:** A symbol of refinement that helps you avoid leaving fingerprints.

3. **Bullet-proof vest:** Absorbs the impact of bullets and betrayals of young protégés.

4. **Ronald Reagan mask:** Hide your identity while showing support for The Gipper.

Swayze Couture Starter Kit

If you'd rather not pay homage to his films, these essential items are all you need in your closet to dress with the cool confidence and relaxed style of everyday Swayze.

1. **Leather jacket:** Naturally distressed and weathered.

2. **Solid color tee:** No patterns needed. Your charming personality says it all.

3. **Denim jeans:** Like Swayze, a classic that never goes out of style.

4. **Cowboy boots**: In case you need to rope cattle before hitting the town.

5. **A smile**: The first accessory everyone notices. You're never fully dressed without it.

Swayze Sutra

Though it may be syllabically similar, Swayze Sutra is not related to that intimately illustrated ancient text. It's a handy assortment of positions and techniques to help make mundane activities seem a little more thrilling. As we've established, Swayze never tried to be a sex symbol, but no matter what he did, he was nothing short of tantalizing. Incorporate these suggestions into your typical solo or partnered activities, and prepare yourself for an abundance of your body's favorite neurotransmitters.

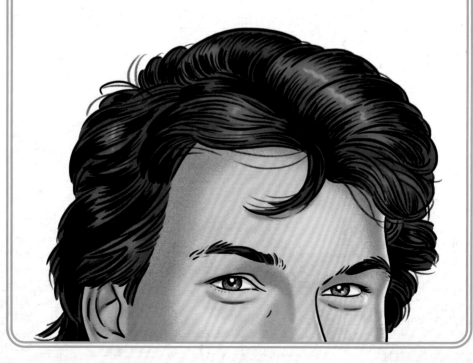

Appropriate Occasions to Go Shirtless

A powerful tool in the sutra is knowing the appropriate time to go shirtless. Swayze didn't have an abundance of bare-chested scenes because, like a good boxer, you don't start the match by throwing your knockout punch. Aside from the obvious, like bathing, intimacy, or contractual obligations, these are a handful of acceptable shirtless moments, à la Patrick Swayze.

- Intently reading Jim Harrison's *Legends of the Fall* by your barn apartment window
- Flossing your tuxedo shirt between your legs during a Chippendales audition
- Putting on your makeup to "I Am the Body Beautiful" by Salt-N-Pepa
- Engaging in a fight to the death, for the throne, on behalf of its rightful king
- Doing your taxes

Choreography for Solo Cleaning

Chores don't always have to be a bore. Next time you're home alone take inspiration from these dance moves that Swayze performed flawlessly, and slightly alter them for your daily duties.

- **Vacuuming:** Perform a rumba box step around a moving Roomba

- **Laundry:** Port de bras or port de boxers to gracefully sort dirty underwear

- **Sweeping**: Slow waltz on lazy Sundays and Viennese waltz if you're expecting company

- **Messy Spills:** Attach a soapy mop to each foot and rand de jambe par terre

- **Dusting:** Arabesque to clean your ceiling fan and hard-to-reach places

Suitable Uses for
Swayzean Eye Contact

Swayze Eyes is a gaze of persuasive power that comes with great responsibility and should only be used sparingly. Masters of this tool find equal success in romantic or reflective situations. It is permissible to Swayze Gaze when . . .

- Looking into your doctor's eyes as she staples your gaping wound

- Watching waves crash on Bells Beach while contemplating your place in this infinite universe

- Staring at your majestic Arabian steed and forming an unbreakable bond

- Intimidating criminals as you deliver federal justice in Chicago

- Dancing to Otis Redding's "These Arms of Mine" or engaging in other "activities"

Quiz: Which Swayze Is Your Soulmate?

When it comes to finding out which iconic Swayze character is your soulmate, forget all the butterflies and possible rejection because all it takes is ten questions and a little imagination. In real life, Swayze didn't need a questionnaire to find his soulmate (that was in a dance class in Houston), but for the rest of us dreamers who had many slumber party debates on this vital and legally binding topic, this quiz will put all those doubts to rest.

1. On top of rock hard abs, a majestic mullet, and that million-dollar smile (which comes standard in every package), your preferred Swayze soulmate must be . . .

    A. Passionate. Experienced. Protective.
    B. Honorable. Courageous. Romantic.
    C. Sensitive. Devoted. Soulful.
    D. Mysterious. Heroic. Independent.

2. You aren't one for "types" because honestly, any Swayze soulmate is ideal. However, if you absolutely had to choose, you'd like your soulmate to be . . .

    A. A little bit country and a little bit rock and roll
    B. A true Southern gentleman
    C. A yuppie with a heart of gold
    D. A noble guardian and wanderer

3. Fashion sense might not be a deal breaker (we're all guilty of sweatpants on the weekend), but this signature look is one you'd never get tired of:

    A. Sexy shades (even indoors), tight pants, leather jacket, black T-shirt

    B. A regal ensemble of a cape, jacket, vest, and, for good measure, an ascot

    C. Formal suits for work; jeans with a colorful button-up (optional) for play

    D. Rugged pants and shirtless vest for optimum muscle tanning real estate

4. On the night of your first date, your soulmate arrives to pick you up with . . .

    A. A motorcycle or sport sedan, depending on the weather

    B. A horse-drawn carriage and blanket

    C. Public transportation—the best way to get around major cities

    D. Nothing. The world is best traveled on foot. Wear comfortable shoes.

5. Since first dates are pivotal to the success of a relationship, you and your soulmate will start the night . . .

    A. At a dance class where the air is humid and full of sexual tension

    B. By taking a romantic pre-dinner stroll through a beautiful garden

    C. Getting your palms read by a fortune-teller before hitting up an art gallery

    D. Stargazing and looking at aqueduct blueprints as you drink pure water

6. At dinner, your soulmate confesses that they have baggage (don't we all?) and hopes that you'll overlook it. You'd have no problem accepting that they . . .

A. Were once treated as a part-time gigolo by lonely vacationing housewives

B. Are conflicted by a tainted family legacy of immoral stances on equality

C. Have difficulties saying, "I love you" despite showing ample affection

D. Have killed many people (who were totally evil!) to protect others

7. As Loverboy taught us in 1981, everybody's working for the weekend. You'd prefer to spend your free weekend afternoon . . .

A. Going for a swim in an ice-cold lake with only each other to keep warm

B. Having a secret rendezvous because you accidentally married someone

C. Watching a classic movie and snuggling in his favorite leather recliner

D. Tenderly watching him act like a father figure to your son

8. Your soulmate's best friend will inevitably be in the picture now. You're content with your social circle but could see yourself making room for their . . .

A. Talented and attractive workmate who knows him better than you

B. Loyal military buddy and occasional Yankee adversary

C. Self-serving colleague who likes to launder more than clothes

D. Weapons. No friends to speak of, but he's sure packing a lot of steel

9. Long-term, fling, rebound—we all have different expectations of relationships. When it comes to your soulmate, the ideal length of your courtship is . . .

    A. Over one season and if Daddy approves, possibly more

    B. Years. Some in-person, some in secret, and some through letters

    C. 'Til death do him part

    D. A fleeting but memorable moment in time

10. When it's time to finally put an end to the will-they-or-won't-they sexual tension and consummate your new relationship, you'll most likely be . . .

    A. Under the romantic glow of paper lanterns and music of Solomon Burke

    B. In an abandoned church (taboo!) where foreplay is removing many layers

    C. Getting dirty on a couch after literally getting dirty in your workshop

    D. In the desert under the stars where kisses (like sand) reach every crevice

Results on Next Page...

YOUR SOULMATE IS:

If you picked mostly As:

You like a bad boy in touch with his feelings. Prepare to have and to hold from this day forward everyone's favorite street-tough-but-sensitive dance instructor Johnny Castle from *Dirty Dancing*. He'll never be sorry, and neither will you.

If you picked mostly Bs:

You like old-fashioned manners and have the patience it takes for true love. For better for worse, for richer or poorer, you're spending your days with soldier Orry Main from *North and South*. But whatever you do, don't let Papa handle the mail.

If you picked mostly Cs:

You like a caring and dependable partner who makes you laugh. You'll share your love with Sam Wheat from *Ghost* in sickness and in health, whether corporeal or not. Keep a few lucky pennies lying around just in case.

If you picked mostly Ds:

You like things casual and exhilarating. After all, it's a post-apocalyptic world! With only so much time to love and to cherish, Nomad from *Steel Dawn* will arrive when you need him most, but he knows when it's time to walk off toward the sunset.

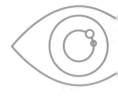

Did You Know?
Fast Facts About *Dirty Dancing*

1. While she insists the story isn't directly based on her life, Screenwriter Eleanor Bergstein certainly embraced the old adage of "write what you know" by taking inspiration from her own family trips to the Catskills, being called "Baby" until she was 20, having a doctor for a father, and yes, doing her own share of dirty dancing too.

2. Director Emile Ardolino had never directed a feature film before *Dirty Dancing*. He did, however, win an Academy Award for Best Documentary for his 1983 movie *He Makes Me Feel Like Dancin'* which landed him the job. Swayze appreciated having a director with a dance background and felt it was integral to the success of the film.

3. Many of the cast and crew thought the film's production was cursed after several instances of bad luck. There was a wave of food poisoning, several broken bones and injuries, flooding, stolen items, quitting crewmembers, and even a wasp infestation that resulted in several stings to star Jennifer Grey's arms.

4. Many of the people involved with the movie, including Swayze, thought the title *Dirty Dancing* would hurt the film's chances of being successful. After some movie executives and the censorship office started to agree, they almost named it *I Was a Teenage Mambo Queen* after Eleanor Bergstein's own experience doing the mambo for contests.

5. After the rough cut of the film was screened for producer Aaron Russo (*Trading Places*) he famously said, "Burn the negative and collect the insurance money" but the filmmakers stuck to their guns, and after some tweaking by Emile Ardolino, it was re-screened for a test audience whose enthusiastic response proved the film would be a hit.

6. During filming, Swayze's old knee injury began to resurface and plagued him throughout the shoot. When Johnny is balancing on the log, it became very painful for Swayze as his bad knee had almost no cartilage left and his bones were grinding on each other. After filming for a few hours, he had to immediately have his knee drained from swelling.

7. Since Swayze's experience as a dancer far exceeded the ability of Johnny Castle, he chose to hold back from incorporating more advanced moves into the film. He did, however, let one fly for fun during the finale when Johnny does an impressive double pirouette after jumping off the stage.

8. The film was shot over 44 days, on a then meager budget of less than $5 Million. When it was released, *Dirty Dancing* became a massive success grossing over $214 Million worldwide, which made it, at the time, the most successful independent film ever made.

9. Swayze first met co-star Jennifer Grey while performing with her father, Joel Grey, on Broadway in *Goodtime Charley* in 1975. They would reconnect on-screen in *Red Dawn*, where a tense relationship began, born out of Swayze being tasked with taking charge of the younger cast members. After initial reservations on Jennifer Grey's part, she and Swayze had a heart-to-heart during the audition for *Dirty Dancing* and the tension mostly drifted away. Whatever differences were left proved to be the necessary ingredients to show passion on-screen that made the film a success.

10. The song "(I've Had) The Time of My Life" was chosen by producer's mere days before the last dance of the film was shot. They, of course, chose wisely and the song would eventually go on to win the Oscar for Best Original Song at the 60th Academy Awards.

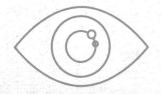

11. Despite the film taking place over summer, the scene between Johnny and Baby practicing the iconic lift in the water was filmed at the end of October making the water, and the weather, "horrifyingly and hypothermically cold" according to Swayze. If you watch closely, you'll notice there are no close-ups of the scene due to the actor's lips beginning to turn blue.

12. With production taking place during autumn, many of the trees on set had to be spray painted green since the leaves were dying or had already changed color.

13. Actress Kelly Bishop was originally cast as Vivian Pressman, the wealthy guest trying to seduce Johnny during dance lessons. When the actress portraying Baby's mother, Marjorie Houseman, fell ill and couldn't continue the production, Bishop stepped in. It proved to be the perfect training for her most famous role as the family matriarch, Emily Gilmore, on *Gilmore Girls*.

14. According to Jennifer Grey, the famous lift at the end of the film was unrehearsed. She only fully performed the lift three times. Once at auditions, once in the water, and once for the finale. Usually practice makes perfect unless you have a perfect dance partner like Swayze who can do it in one take.

15. Swayze's wife, Lisa Niemi, was at the auditions and helped demonstrate certain maneuvers to make Jennifer Grey feel at ease. She also auditioned for the role of Penny Johnson, which ultimately went to actress Cynthia Rhodes.

Element 4:

Peaceful WARRIOR

LESSON NO. 4:
Find your code of honor and live by it

The fourth element in saluting Swayze is called Peaceful Warrior, and it highlights Swayze's fascination with Eastern philosophy that informed many of his performances. It also represents a character with exceptional physical prowess hidden behind an unbreakable Zen-like code. Audiences have had their fair share of tried-and-true heroic archetypes to admire on the big screen, from reluctant heroes like Ellen Ripley, anti-heroes like "Dirty" Harry Callahan, or even vengeful heroes like John Wick, but missing from every list is the Peaceful Warrior, a character played to perfection by Swayze, cementing him in cinema history as the ultimate deep-thinking tough guy.

The Swayze Code

East Meets Old West

Whether he knew it or not, Swayze imbued his characters with an unrivaled spiritual equilibrium and philosophical code that took otherwise one-note characters on the page and transformed them into fully fleshed-out heroes and villains on the screen. Perhaps these principles can be traced back to his self-described melting-pot belief system. Born out of a passion for researching the many ways people find hope and faith, he combined his studies with the various tenets of the martial arts he trained in like Wushu, Taekwondo, and Aikido, to name a few. After studying Mahayana Buddhism for many years, he would often joke that the best way to know how he was doing was to check the condition of his butsudan (the altar where he chanted) and you'd get your answer. In other words, the cleaner the altar, the clearer the mind. This unique influence has perhaps never been as strong as in the words of his characters like Zen surfer Bodhi (*Point Break),* pacifist bouncer Dalton (*Road House),* or saintly drifter Jack McCloud (*Three Wishes).* Those descriptions may sound like oxymorons, but what made Swayze special was that he leaned into contradictory character profiles by inserting philosophical or spiritual subtext, and through those added principles evoked traits of successful cinematic counterparts in the East.

A character like Bodhi in a typical actor's hands would have been your run-of-the-mill robber and foil for our hero to easily defeat. Swayze's preparation and dedication are fully on display here as he creates a magnetic multilayered character (a spiritual adrenaline junkie disguising his moral cowardice) that jumps off the screen with an almost mystical allure. He's not a monologuing

Bond villain or an irredeemable antagonist of pure evil, but a charismatic leader . . . who also happens to be a criminal. Halfway through the film even Johnny Utah almost succumbs to the cult of Bodhi and his hypnotic unyielding beliefs. It works flawlessly because Swayze refuses to wink at the audience. A masterful choice he birthed on *Road House*, the cult movie legend and king of "so bad it's good" movies, where bouncers are like gunslingers and their fists are like six-shooters.

Swayze wholeheartedly embraced the classic Americana backdrop and eighties acid-wash dialogue of *Road House*. Exuding a meditative calmness, he delivered a sincere performance, despite his character existing in a pseudo–Old West fictional world of gratuitous nudity and gorilla presses to the tune of hard blues. He was so convincing, in fact, that twenty-five years later his "three simple rules" scene was used by the NYPD (yes, *that* NYPD) for a mandatory retraining course on how to behave in the field. Some might reduce Rowdy Herrington's 1989 film to one giant bar fight of fun, but it afforded Swayze a few key things: It allowed him to flex his action muscles and throw roundhouse kicks before his knee gave out; homage stoic characters like The Man with No Name and Sanjuro; and most of all, the chance to play a monk-like drifter (with a code of honor) who conveniently fights like Bruce Lee. Swayze took roles that today would be seen as larger than life and simply made them work. Zen or not, that makes him a master.

Have a Bodhi Day
A Schedule for Maximum Bodhictivity

Absorb and appreciate Bodhi's routine and you, too, will learn to take on habits that will alleviate stress, and allow you to flourish.

5:30am — Wake up. Wax surfboard and any excess body hair. Wet suit-up

6:03am — Marvel at the sunrise and appreciate how small and fragile we are in the grand scheme of things

6:15am — Dance with the universe a.k.a. go surfing at Latigo Beach

9:30am — Send Roach to dry clean suits and sanitize masks

9:45am — Practice dog psychology in the mirror

10:00am — Journal about every wave that had the pleasure of you riding on it

11:00am — Double check Grommet's parachute packing skills

11:30am — Uncover the newest getaway car and tune it to your favorite radio station

1:30pm — Take a quick dip in the ocean and bathe under the sun

4:00pm — Hire a fire-breather for the nightly shindig

5:00pm — Light an obscene amount of candles

7:30pm — Party. Eat. Drink. Dance. Party. Repeat

10:30pm — Help Rosie set up a bonfire on the beach

10:45pm — Spit wisdom over the fire while stringing a guitar

12:00am — Nocturnal surf session

1:00am — Plan and organize newest "financial venture"

1:15am — Drift away to a peaceful sleep under the watchful eye of the moon

The Virtues of Bodhi

Aim to achieve a similar state of mind as everyone's favorite surfing mentor by following this handful of obtainable virtues.

Stay True to Your Crew

Family doesn't always mean blood. Find that tight-knit group of friends who have no problem playing pick-up football on the beach, jumping out of a perfectly good airplane, or playing dress-up for 90 seconds while engaging in nefarious activities. You're never alone with a squad of loyal ride or dies.

Respect Mother Nature

Mother Nature will not be manipulated or understood. She'll destroy you without hesitation. Even world-class athletes with immaculate beards and gorgeous sun kissed locks aren't impervious to her wicked ways. If you want to simultaneously lose yourself and find yourself, you must surrender, and accept her energy.

Always Be Searching

Life isn't about playing it safe. It's about taking risks. It's about searching for the ultimate ride in every situation. Because life, that cruel cosmic game with a sick sense of humor, only has a finite number of players. So when the little hand says it's time to rock and roll, embrace the invitation, and play the game.

Rage Against the System

Society is too content existing as a bunch of dead souls inching along the freeway inside a metal coffin. Work isn't about the monotony of a 9-5. It's about shaking up the status quo, reviving the human spirit, and getting a rush for four months out of the year so you can party for the remaining eight.

Your Body Is a Temple

Like a surfboard, your body is a work of art. Spend the time to properly shape it so you become the best version of yourself, inside your wet suit, and out. Eat healthy, and if you must drink, do so in moderation. Unless it's tequila. In that case, only ingest alongside a fresh lime wedge and puka shell-wearing dance partner.

Self-Guided Swayzeness

Swayze was a globe-trotting superstar with a jam-packed schedule, and like many of his characters, he found time to meditate. Whether you're just beginning or close to enlightenment, the health benefits of meditation have been well documented. But as with anything, without practice, they won't work. It's time to train your mind to find peace and calm in any situation by completing these character-guided meditation sessions inspired by Swayze's most mindful performances.

So put away your noise-canceling headphones and aromatherapy candles, because the only tool you'll need is your mind. Read each prompt, close your eyes, and let these scenarios transport you away to your very own Zen mindscape.

Jack McCloud and the Hitchhiker's Guide to Meditation

Visualize sitting on the pitcher's mound of a Little League baseball field. The air is a mixture of freshly popped popcorn, wildflowers, and sweat-soaked polyester. Disregard any suggestive glances from 1950s housewives and instead focus on the warmth of the sun as it rejuvenates your skin and sparkles on your perfectly manicured beard.

The Fragrance of Nature According to Dalton

You're in a beautiful barn apartment with spacious windows. Rent is one hundred dollars a month (it's the eighties), and despite no phone, television, or conditioned air, it's peaceful tranquility. Ignore the raucous rotor blades of the villainous business magnate's helicopter across the pond. Getting centered is more important than dishing out obscene gestures of violence.

Full Bodhi Relaxation

Picture yourself at the beach. Crackling fire.
Crashing waves. What do you smell?
Is it the salty sea air or shrimp and fries?
Coconut body butter or two meatball subs?
As opportunistic seagulls swarm above your
head, take a deep breath and remember that
surfing's the source and it can change your life.
Good waves, good vibes, good times.

Nomadic Nirvana

In order to achieve balance through meditation, you must first meditate while you balance . . . on your head. Imagine you're in the desert and feel the weight of gravity pressing down on your spine as blood rushes to your head. The ever-shifting sand dunes sing a song of time passing by as tiny creatures crawl beside you and join the steady hum.

Congratulations! You have now reached Swayzean levels of spiritual awareness. As you carve out your own path in life, remember to live in the present, ignore any negative energy, and, most importantly, breathe.

Nama-Swayze, friends.

Did You Know?
Fast Facts About *Ghost*

1. Tony Goldwyn's wife, successful production designer Jane Musky, happened to be working on *Ghost* and noticed that the role of Sam's villainous best friend Carl hadn't been cast yet. She pushed him to audition and in turn, he received his big break.

2. *Ghost* was the highest-grossing film of 1990 pulling in over $200 Million dollars domestically and eventually surpassing $500 Million around the globe. The film notably beat out *Pretty Woman* and Macaulay Culkin's holiday juggernaut *Home Alone* for the top spot.

3. Tony Goldwyn was so convincing as a villain that after the film was released, going out in public just wasn't the same. In New York City, while he was on a break from play rehearsals, he was often refused a seat at restaurants or the recipient of dirty looks from strangers in public who just couldn't explain why they didn't like him.

4. Take a recording of a baby crying, reverse it, and play it back in slow motion if you want to recreate the haunting sound that the shadowy demons make when they capture evil souls in the film. That's how the filmmakers did it!

5. Demi Moore's famous hairstyle from the film was a complete surprise to the filmmakers. During her audition, Moore's hair was long and curly, and without telling anyone, she showed up to set on the first day sporting her then influential "boy cut" courtesy of famed celebrity hairstylist John Sahag.

6. Patrick Swayze had yet another uphill battle to win the part of Sam Wheat. After he expressed interest in the role, director Jerry Zucker walked out of a screening of *Road House* with Bruce Joel Rubin and said "Over my dead body" thinking

Swayze couldn't pull off the tender role. After a lengthy audition process, Swayze won over Zucker and proved he was more than a tough guy.

7. During the horrific scene when Sam is watching Molly hold his dead body, the first takes captured were unusable due to such a visceral reaction from Swayze. The prosthetic dummy that Demi Moore was holding (cast of his own body) eerily looked like his father the day of his funeral. With it all flashing back, he couldn't contain his emotions.

8. *Ghost* was actually Jerry Zucker's first solo venture into directing after serving as co-director on comedy classics like *Airplane!*, *The Naked Gun*, and *Top Secret*. Screenwriter Bruce Joel Rubin famously admitted that when he heard that the director of *Airplane!* was going to direct his script, he cried. Those tears were quickly dried as the dynamic duo collaborated to make one of the most loved films of all time.

9. The filmmakers originally conceived Molly as a woodworker, but thought the image of her hammering and chiseling away at large blocks of wood wasn't the right fit for the film. Molly eventually became a potter after Jerry Zucker saw a pottery magazine on his sound editor's desk while working on *The Naked Gun* and realized the potential it had for dramatic, and of course, sensual purposes.

10. The idea for *Ghost* came to Bruce Joel Rubin after he watched a production of *Hamlet*. When the ghost of Hamlet's father asks him to avenge his murder, Rubin thought it would be interesting to expand on that concept for 20th century America, and thus, the idea was born.

11. The film, and of course Swayze's amazing performance, had a surprising influence on the hip-hop world as the term "Swayze" or "Ghost like Swayze" has since been used in countless rhymes by artists like 2Pac, Jay-Z, The Notorious B.I.G., and even The Lonely Island on their SNL Digital Short masterpiece, "Lazy Sunday." Later in life Swayze embraced

his popularity in hip-hop by appearing in the music video for Ja Rule's "Murder Reigns" as a detective.

12. Shows like *Two and a Half Men*, *Community,* and *Family Guy* are just a few of the shows, among countless others, that have parodied the famous pottery scene. Jerry Zucker's own brother David poked fun of him when he directed a recreation in *The Naked Gun 2 ½: The Smell of Fear*, but perhaps the funniest parody belongs to famed BFF's Martha Stewart and Snoop Dogg who iced a chocolate cake to the tune of "Unchained Melody" as a promo for their reality show.

13. When she auditioned for the film, Demi Moore impressed everyone with her amazing ability to seemingly produce tears on demand. It sure came in handy for this film.

14. In order to achieve certain special effect shots of ghost Sam throwing punches through bodies or fighting with Carl, the filmmakers used a motion control rig which is designed to film specific camera movements and timings for repeated takes so that they can then be spliced together. Swayze would hit all of his marks exactly in time with the choreography, they would film it again without him or with other actors, and when they were put together it seemed like they were interacting in the same space.

15. Director Jerry Zucker and Bruce Joel Rubin went through 19 drafts of the script to find the exact right tone between the thriller, romance, and comedic aspects of the story.

Swayze
or Philosopher?

Now that you fully understand Swayze's affinity for portraying philosophically inclined characters with witty and thought-provoking quips, it's time to put that knowledge to the test! Do you think you'd be able to recognize the difference between something Swayze said and a quote from an actual philosopher? This final test of wits is all that stands between you and the title of Peaceful Warrior, and the best part is, you didn't have to bust any heads along the way!

Swayze or Philosopher?
Circle your answer!

1. And those who were seen dancing were thought to be insane by those who could not hear the music.   **S P**

2. If you want the ultimate, you've got to be willing to pay the ultimate price. It's not tragic to die doing what you love.   **S P**

3. Perfect numbers, like perfect men, are very rare.   **S P**

4. I don't know why we are here, but I'm pretty sure it is not in order to enjoy ourselves.   **S P**

5. You don't just stop living because you lose someone.   S   P

6. The only meaning of life worth caring about is one that can withstand our best efforts to examine it.   S   P

7. With love and patience, nothing is impossible.   S   P

8. Fear causes hesitation, and hesitation will cause your worst fears to come true.   S   P

9. Believe in yourself, imagine good things, and moisturize.   S   P

10. Man is the only creature who refuses to be what he is.   S   P

11. The mountains pay us no attention at all. You laugh or you cry . . . the wind just keeps on blowin'.   S   P

12. You ask a philosopher a question, and after he or she has talked for a bit, you don't understand your question anymore.   S   P

13. The only way to make sense out of change is to plunge into it, move with it, and join the dance.   S   P

14. We all lose things. Every day. Some things are so small we hardly notice. Others hurt. A lot. If we don't give up, we'll get to see that we're always getting something else instead.   S   P

15. There's no way of proving that I won't fail in combat. But then again, you can't prove that I will, either.   S   P

16. People understand me so poorly that they don't even understand my complaint about them not understanding me.   **S P**

17. Why be a servant to the law, when you can be its master?   **S P**

18. If you push too hard at anything, you'll get the exact opposite of what you're trying for. Everything contains its opposite.   **S P**

19. You will never do anything in this world without courage. It is the greatest quality of the mind next to honor.   **S P**

20. I look in the mirror, and all I see is a young old man with only a dream.   **S P**

ANSWERS

1. Philosopher (Friedrich Nietzsche)

2. Swayze (Bodhi, *Point Break*)

3. Philosopher (René Descartes)

4. Philosopher (Ludwig Wittgenstein)

5. Swayze (Darrel "Darry" Curtis, *The Outsiders*)

6. Philosopher (Daniel Dennett)

7. Philosopher (Daisaku Ikeda)

8. Swayze (Bodhi, *Point Break*)

9. Swayze (Vida Boheme, *To Wong Foo, Thanks For Everything! Julie Newmar*)

10. Philosopher (Albert Camus)

11. Swayze (Jed Eckert, *Red Dawn*)

12. Philosopher (Philippa Foot)

13. Philosopher (Alan Watts)

14. Swayze (Jack McCloud, *Three Wishes*)

15. Swayze (Kevin Scott, *Uncommon Valor*)

16. Philosopher (Søren Kierkegaard)

17. Swayze (Bodhi, *Point Break*)

18. Swayze (Jack McCloud, *Three Wishes*)

19. Philosopher (Aristotle)

20. Swayze (Himself, lyrics from "She's Like the Wind")

Element 5:

The MULLET

LESSON NO. 5:
Write a legacy that can't be erased

The fifth and final element in celebrating Swayze is influenced by and named after the true source of his power: The Mullet. Despite his love/hate relationship with this hairstyle, it perfectly represents his long-lasting legacy. Whether fans have followed his career for months, years, or just started with this book, the continued respect for Swayze highlights the indelible mark he left on popular culture. His enduring work inspired countless fan groups, yearly dancing contests, tours, experiences, and even humorous interactive stage plays based on his films. And yet, it won't be Johnny Castle or Sam Wheat remembered as his greatest performance, for that honor belongs to the role he played in fighting cancer. The Mullet may just be a symbol, but Swayze's power keeping us glued to our screens and giving hope to those fighting similar battles will not soon be forgotten.

The Swayze Legacy

One Last Ride into the Sunset

Swayze often remarked that his work was his legacy and it's clear that his projects reflected who he was as a person. He made films about family, friendships, self-discovery, connecting with the universe, and seizing every moment we have on this earth. He championed female filmmakers, took chances on unproven talent, and stood by his passion for the story being paramount to any project. Swayze truly embodied the phrase "live life to the fullest" and after cheating death many times, he lived every day as if it was his last. Certainly this is a perspective we could all benefit from.

Besides singing, dancing, and perfectly toned muscles, at his core Swayze was also a true conservationist. His love for Mother Nature was just as strong as his love for animals. He worked tirelessly to save enough money to build a ranch (known as Rancho Bizarro) with his wife, Lisa, so they could create a private life away from the noise of Hollywood. Their California property allowed the soulmates to raise their beloved horses, care for their loyal dogs and various pets, and be closer to the wilderness, a constant reminder of Swayze's deep Texas roots but also a soul rejuvenator in between projects. His environmental work near their New Mexico property (relocating the Gallinas river to improve the local habitat) proved that his legacy was more than just artistic contributions.

Swayze was known as "Buddy" to friends and family, which is fitting because, to millions of fans, he was their buddy—a friendly face that made them laugh, cry, and most of all, feel. Those same fans rallied around Swayze when he was diagnosed with pancreatic cancer in 2008. He fought this disease for twenty straight months, even filming an entire TV series (*The Beast*) while undergoing chemotherapy. He ultimately lost his battle, but for many others the war continues to rage on. He never wanted to be the poster child for pancreatic cancer, but his courage under fire (and quest for a cure and awareness) serves as an inspiration. Swayze once said, "I dream that the word 'cure' will no longer be followed by the words 'it's impossible.'" He lived an incredibly full and passionate life (more lifetimes than most ever will), and if there's one thing he taught us, it's that impossible doesn't exist. If you try hard enough, love hard enough, and dream big enough, like Swayze, you can conquer anything.

To donate or learn more about taking action against pancreatic cancer, visit the Pancreatic Cancer Action Network (PanCAN) at www.pancan.org.

The Best of Swayze

Feast your eyes on this collection of top five lists covering the best-of Swayze moments with trivia tidbits in between. This partial and by no means definitive list covers all aspects of his career and serves as a celebratory dedication to the man that inspired them.

Best Character Names

Honorable Mention:
Ace Johnson

(Skatetown, U.S.A.)

5. Truman Gates

(Next of Kin)

4. Bodhi

(Point Break)*

3. Race Darnell

(Letters from a Killer)

2. Velvet Larry

(Powder Blue)

1. Vida Boheme

(To Wong Foo, Thanks for Everything! Julie Newmar)

* Bodhi is short for "Bodhisattva," or an enlightened being who, out of compassion, forgoes nirvana in order to save others.

Best Television Roles

Honorable Mention:
Bandit

(The Renegades)*

5. Allan Quartermain

(King Solomon's Mines)

4. Eric David Peterson

(Amazing Stories, "Life on Death Row")

3. Private Gary Sturgis

(M*A*S*H, "Blood Brother")

2. Charles Barker

(The Beast)

1. Orry Main

(North and South, Book I & II)

* The day Swayze landed the lead role, he called wife Lisa Niemi from inside a DeLorean dealership, where he had just purchased one of their cars.

Best Movie Taglines

Honorable Mention: "The ice...The fire...
The fight...To be the best."

(Youngblood)

5. "In our time, no foreign army has ever
occupied American soil. Until now."

(Red Dawn)*

4. "Don't open the mail."

(Letters from a Killer)

3. "The dancing's over. Now it gets dirty."

(Road House)

2. "27 banks in three years—anything to
catch the perfect wave!"

(Point Break)

1. "He's America's most wanted . . . Dad!"

(Father Hood)

** As if the movie weren't explosive enough, Swayze used to play
epic pranks on set like taping mini-explosives under the personal
toilet of director John Milius.*

Best Modes of Transportation

Honorable Mention: Dennis Jarvis Custom Spyder Surfboard

*(Point Break)**

5. 1972 Cadillac Fleetwood Eldorado

(Father Hood)

4. 1994 Peterbilt 379

(Black Dog)

3. 1957 Chevrolet Bel Air Sport Coupe

(Dirty Dancing)

2. 1968 Plymouth Road Runner

(Tiger Warsaw)

1. A Tornado

(Tall Tale)

* Sold at auction for $64,000. Talk about paying the ultimate price!

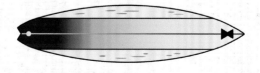

Best On-Screen Chemistry

Honorable Mention: Kristin Scott Thomas

(Keeping Mum)

5. Wesley Snipes/John Leguizamo

(To Wong Foo, Thanks for Everything! Julie Newmar)

4. Lisa Niemi

(Steel Dawn, One Last Dance)

3. Kelly Lynch

(Road House)

2. Demi Moore/Whoopi Goldberg

(Ghost)*

1. Jennifer Grey

(Dirty Dancing)

* Whoopi Goldberg has said that Swayze told producers if they didn't cast her as Oda Mae Brown, he wouldn't do the movie. Her performance in the film would go on to win the Academy Award for Best Supporting Actress. Screenwriter Bruce Joel Rubin also took home a statue for Best Original Screenplay.

Most Eligible Wingman

Honorable Mention:
Roger Aaron Brown/Oliver Platt

(Tall Tale)

5. Charlie Sheen

(Red Dawn)

4. C. Thomas Howell

(The Outsiders, Grandview, U.S.A., Red Dawn)*

3. Sam Elliott

(Road House)

2. Keanu Reeves

(Point Break and Youngblood)

1. Rob Lowe

(Youngblood and The Outsiders)

* Swayze and Howell became good buddies after their triple collaboration. They both shared a love of horses, calf-roping, and all things cowboy.

Best Kisses

Honorable Mention: Slam & Mike

(Grandview, U.S.A.)

5. Allan Quartermain & Elizabeth Maitland

(King Solomon's Mines)

4. Johnny & Baby

(Dirty Dancing)

3. Nomad & Kasha

(Steel Dawn)

2. Orry & Madeline

(North and South)

1. Ghost Sam & Molly

(Ghost)*

* In 2008, Denplan (the UK's leading dental plan) commissioned a survey asking people about their favorite cinematic kisses in honor of National Kissing Day. The top spot went to none other than Swayze and Demi Moore for Ghost. *He even nabbed third place with Jennifer Grey for* Dirty Dancing, *cementing him as cinema's best on-screen kisser.*

Most Acceptable Times to Yell "Wolverines!"

Honorable Mention: Sitting in your car after doing your civic duty and voting

5. After kissing a coed under the Engineering Arch at University of Michigan*

4. On top of rock formations or at the Top of the Rock Observation Deck (NYC)

3. Answering "Whose cigar is this?" at Xavier's School for Gifted Youngsters

2. When browsing Etsy and spotting wool figurines of entertainer Ben Vereen

1. At all *Red Dawn* film screenings and watch parties

* *You're guaranteed a high five if you utter this anywhere in Ann Arbor.*

Most Unacceptable Times to Yell "Wolverines!"

Honorable Mention:
When Hugh Jackman is taking a nap*

5. While participating in the annual Mirror Lake Jump at Ohio State University

4. Reading the specials at a fancy restaurant

3. During the annual shareholder meeting of The Timberland Company

2. In the audience at The Christian Siriano Collection at New York Fashion Week

1. Inside a Canadian daycare center

* The most hardworking man in show business deserves a few hours of shut-eye.

Best Dance Performances

Honorable Mention:
Rumba with Whoopi Goldberg

(Whoopi, *"The Last Dance"*)

5. Channeling *Saturday Night Fever* in a 1979 Pabst Blue Ribbon commercial

4. Oozing sex appeal during a solo roller skate dance

(*Skatetown, U.S.A.*)

3. The Chippendales Audition sketch

(*SNL, S16E4*)

2. 1994 World Music Awards with Lisa Niemi

1. Every hip thrust, ball change, spin, and lift!

(*Dirty Dancing*)*

The film was choreographed by Emmy-winning choreographer/ director Kenny Ortega, who, following the film, would go on to direct such films as Newsies, Hocus Pocus, *and* The High School Musical Trilogy, *as well as reuniting with Swayze on* To Wong Foo, Thanks For Everything! Julie Newmar.

Best Fight Scenes

Honorable Mention:
Socs vs. Greasers Rumble

*(The Outsiders)**

5. Jack vs. Cutler

(Black Dog)

4. Sailor vs. Scott

(Uncommon Valor)

3. Ghost Sam Wheat vs. Carl

(Ghost)

2. Bodhi vs. Johnny Utah

(Point Break)

1. Dalton vs. Jimmy

(Road House)

* If you'd like to see the actual Curtis Brothers' house, located a block away from where the rumble took place, head over to 731 N St. Louis Avenue in Tulsa, Oklahoma, to visit The Outsiders House Museum. Danny Boy O'Connor, founding member of hip-hop group House of Pain and noted super fan of The Outsiders, *bought and renovated the house to preserve the film's legacy and its contributions to the city of Tulsa.*

Corners Nobody Should Put Baby In*

Honorable Mention:
The House at Pooh Corner

5. A teashop inglenook in Bath next to a copy of "In a Bath Teashop" by John Betjeman

4. Four Corners Monument (Arizona, Colorado, New Mexico, Utah)

3. Pre-1970, "The Masta Kink"; Post-1970, "Maggotts, Becketts, and Chapel"

2. Next to Michael Stipe, in the corner, under the spotlight, losing religion

1. The Corner, both literally and figuratively

Swayze initially hated the line "Nobody puts Baby in a corner," until he saw the finished cut of Dirty Dancing and admitted it worked. It was one instance where he was happy to be wrong, as this iconic line is not only a part of popular culture but was included on AFI's list of The 100 Greatest Movie Quotes of All Time.

Best Swayze Performance

Honorable Mention:

5.

4.

3.

2.

1. Trick Question. Obviously, it's all of them.

St. Patrick Swayze Day

AUGUST 18TH

The National Day Calendar tracks nearly fifteen hundred national days, weeks, and months, covering such time-honored national traditions as Mascot Day, Get Funky Day, and everyone's perennial favorite, Rhubarb Vodka Day. One holiday sorely missing from this exhaustive list is St. Patrick Swayze Day, or Swayze's birthday, which falls on August 18th. Turn this otherwise ordinary day into an epic birthday celebration by swapping the cake and candles for one of these ten Swayze-inspired activities and experiences to honor him.

1. Learn a new skill like surfing, guitar, or how to pilot a twin-engine Cessna.

2. Travel somewhere unfamiliar to explore and appreciate new cultures.

3. Practice self-care with a new diet, workout plan, or mental-health routine.

4. Write a longhand letter to someone you love or admire.

5. Conquer one of your fears like skydiving or public speaking.

6. Support live theater by seeing a play, musical, or drag show.

7. Enroll in a martial arts program, pottery class, or take a dance lesson.

8. Go horseback riding and became one with nature.

9. Donate blood, and when they insert the needle say, "pain don't hurt."

10. Throw a party for the uninitiated, featuring a biographical slideshow, Swayze double feature, and a copy of this very handbook for further study.

Match the Mullet to the Movie

The sheer power of Swayze's essence created the elements we now use to celebrate him, but it is also responsible for the magical properties that helped transform any cut or style he wore (regardless of what it actually was) into an honorary Mullet. It's time to confirm your ultimate Swayzean devotion by matching illustrations of on-screen Mullets with the project in which they appeared. Once this test is complete, you will officially be crowned a certified practitioner of Feng Swayze, duty bound to proselytize for St. Patrick, and indoctrinate the uninformed masses on the legacy of the master of the Mullet.

1. *Ghost*
2. *Dirty Dancing*
3. *Youngblood*
4. *Red Dawn*
5. *Road House*
6. *Point Break*
7. *North and South*
8. *Black Dog*
9. *George and the Dragon*
10. *Donnie Darko*

A. The Newton John Sweatband Insurgency

B. The Attitudinal Quiff

C. Call Me the Love Mane

D. Surf Wax Poetic

E. Highway Cuttery

F. New Town, Same Style

G. The Palmetto Gentelman

H. A Righteous Trimming

I. Luscious Lettuce

J. Alice in Chainmail

ANSWERS

1. Ghost
H. A righteous Trimming

2. Dirty Dancing
C. Call Me the Love Mane

3. Youngblood
I. Luscious Lettuce

4. Red Dawn
A. The Newton John Sweatband Insurgency

5. Road House
F. New Town, Same Style

6. Point Break
D. Surf Wax Poetic

7. North and South
G. The Palmetto Gentelman

8. Black Dog
E. Highway Cuttery

9. George and the Dragon
J. Alice in Chainmail

10. Donnie Darko
B. The Attitudinal Quiff

Congratulations!

Your training in the art of Feng Swayze is now complete! You've successfully acquired a Tender Strength, exhibited Pure Adrenaline, activated your Hungry Eyes, transformed into a Peaceful Warrior, and properly appreciated The Mullet. You may be wondering...what kind of prize do I receive for passing this course? A certificate? A merit badge? Participatory trophy?

None of the above. Because atop that marvelous noggin of yours is the only prize you'll ever need. You are now the proud owner of your very own metaphorical mullet and are expected, nay, obligated, to rock that newfound confidence with all the Swayzean swagger you can muster till it's time to ride your last wave. All you have to do is follow one simple rule:

Live each and every day like it's your last. Why? Because that's the Swayze way.

Acknowledgments

As I sit here writing this in the backseat of my car listening to a "café noises" playlist on my headphones, my partner-in-crime Colleen is driving us back from a spontaneous seven-hour jaunt to Nashville. She's awesome like that. We went to see the epic Swayze mural on the side of The Centennial Bar so I would have the coolest author photo imaginable. This experience makes me realize that writing in a moving car isn't quite as romantic as a typewriter in Paris, but when you get to pass signs for things like the world's largest pocketknife and "Rest Area 1 Mile" you know you've made it. Truth be told, this was always going to be the hardest for me to write because if you know me, you know I'm the type of person who needs to thank everyone until there's nobody left, or in the dream scenario, John Williams plays me off. But I'll give it a go. As a filmmaker, I learned quickly that while auteur theory is fun to study, no project exists without a team of collaborators and supporters. So, despite my name being on the cover, I want everyone to know you were integral to my success at conceiving, writing, and finishing this book.

Like Tilghman in *Road House*, the only reason my vision was protected was due to a talented team of badass bouncers working to make me look good. Assembling that crew was the best cooler in the business, and editor extraordinaire, Rebecca Hunt. Getting to work with you on this journey makes me even more excited for the next one. You embraced my overwriting, and whether using them or not, always appreciated my incessant pop culture references. If you enjoyed flipping through each page, and like me, marveled at the design, you can thank Maggie Edelman for her incredible work and apparent superpower of hearing my inner thoughts. Just like *What Women Want*. Sorry, Becca! Lynda Crawford, you are the sole reason I don't have to worry about former English teachers calling me out in public. Kyle Hilton, I knew it would take a supremely talented artist to render a subject like Swayze, who is practically chiseled from the Gods, and you far exceeded my expectations. And to all the staff at Chronicle Books that touched this project, from assistants to management, I'm grateful for your hard work and am still amazed and thankful you decided to take a chance on this pop culture nerd.

Bill Gladstone and the team at Waterside Productions Inc., you've been essential to the success of this project. Seth Nagel and Jon Katzman, you believed in this idea the moment I made an off-handed comment about it. If you hadn't, the parking ticket I got that day would be the wrong kind of souvenir.

Lisa Niemi, you have been a constant source of inspiration. I hope I did you and Patrick proud. And to Deirdre Radler, who I'm happy to now call a friend, I couldn't have done this without all the encouraging phone calls and support.

Mom, Dad, David, Papa, Grandma, and Fafa, I'm so incredibly lucky that a loving and supportive family is the one constant in my life. Thank you, Auntie Ann, for playing the VHS of *Youngblood* on repeat when you watched me as a little kid. If you hadn't, this book wouldn't exist. Aria and Ivy, you can't read this yet, but know that you keep me young by making me feel like the coolest uncle around. To the entire Stahnke family, you've made me feel like one of you from day one. I'm honored to have you in my life. To the rest of my family near and far, I love you. And to Colleen, the strongest person I know, it would take 144 more pages to properly express my love for you. I'm excited for a lifetime of traveling the world in search of cute coffee shops.

Justin Shady, on top of being a mentor, anger translator, and friend, your hatred of widows at the end of paragraphs rubbed off on me like glitter from a greeting card. Phil Platakis, the Wade to my Dalton, your input was invaluable, and if I didn't say it out loud..."I'm saying it now." To all my friends, thanks for the support and messages about the book's progress, and for answering my oddball questions for inspiration. To Ken, Matt, and Jeff of Triviality, thank you for being great podcast partners and members of *Pain Don't Hurt*. To the awesome listeners of Triviality, thanks for indulging my weekly mentions of *Road House* and still deciding to listen and support the show.

Rapid-fire shout outs to Carmen Aiello, David Dye and Mercer County, PA, Annette and Kyle Chase, Radar Studios, *The Great British Bake Off*, The Shake Boys, *Ted Lasso*, walks with Max, James Baum for barhopping, Tiger Balm, Diane Marelli and Kevin McOlgan for making me believe in myself, Julia and Lauren of Miss Information Podcast, David Nevarez for lifting me to new heights, Six Dorks Productions, Derek Mungor for always being a set of eyes, and too many more to name. To all the contributors of quotes or blurbs, I was already a fan, but now I'm an even bigger one.

In honor of Patrick, I'd like to make one more dedication to a group of loved ones lost to cancer. Roxanne Barone and Tony Pawlik, I'm grateful to have spent time with you. Tony Montague, I miss singing Tenacious D together. And to our beloved Aunt Teruko, who successfully imparted her kindness to everyone she met, I miss your laugh, and your hugs. Like Patrick, I hope one day a cure for this disease won't be deemed impossible.

About the Author

Mural by I Saw the Sign

Neal E. Fischer is an award-winning filmmaker, writer, and pop culture fanatic patiently waiting on The Criterion Collection to wake up and include Patrick Swayze's *Road House* in their catalog. Directly inspired by Swayze's creative versatility at a young age, Neal cut his teeth as a musician and performer on stage before ultimately transitioning behind the scenes. After a brief but rewarding stint directing children's theatre in Chicago's South Loop, Neal moved on to a diverse slate of projects like the award-winning documentary *10 Mountains 10 Years*, narrated by Anne Hathaway, *#WhoKilledHeather*, an innovative branded web series, and many short films and features screened at festivals around the world. When he's not writing or developing film and television projects, Neal spends his time directing national commercials for brands such as Dunkin' Donuts, Wisconsin Lottery, TD Ameritrade, and Cars.com, the latter of which was shortlisted for awards at Cannes Lions and was his first Super Bowl campaign.

You can hear Neal's bad impressions and obscure movie references each week on Triviality, a pub-trivia-style podcast recorded under the watchful eye of its patron saint of podcasting, Patrick Swayze, whose poster proudly hangs in the studio. His love for entertainment comes from his mom, and despite watching movies many would deem inappropriate for a five-year-old, the mere existence of this bio proves that Neal turned out just fine.

If you'd like to learn more about Neal or see a dated video of him performing the iconic lift from *Dirty Dancing*, you can visit www.nealefischer.com.